SECRET NEW ORLEANS

A GUIDE TO THE WEIRD, WONDERFUL, AND OBSCURE

Mark Aspiazu, James Corbyn, and Angela Papke Aspiazu

Reedy Press
PO Box 5131
St. Louis, MO 63139
www.reedypress.com

Library of Congress Control Number: 2019952741

ISBN: 9781681062181

Design by Jill Halpin

Printed in the United States of America
20 21 22 23 24 5 4 3 2 1

From Angela:
To my family, for supporting whatever crazy thing I throw myself into. To the love of my life, Mark, who makes absolutely every experience awesome and magical. I can't imagine exploring, enduring, and celebrating life without you! And to the beautiful gumbo pot of people in New Orleans who persevere through every catastrophe and obstacle in order to preserve their unique traditions and second line another day.

From James:
To Christina, Rachel, and Dan, for deciding to come on this grand adventure with me. To Darja, who inspires me to be both a better writer and a better person. And to Ruby, my wife: your love is the best secret I've ever discovered, and without your support none of this would be possible.
I love you.

From Mark:
For my son, Mark Aspiazu, Jr., who is always ready to seek out the newest New Orleans secrets with me. For my parents, Hernando and Gina Aspiazu, who raised me to love this amazing city. For my partner in life and adventure, Angela, who is always one step ahead of me when there's something new to explore. We've only just begun.

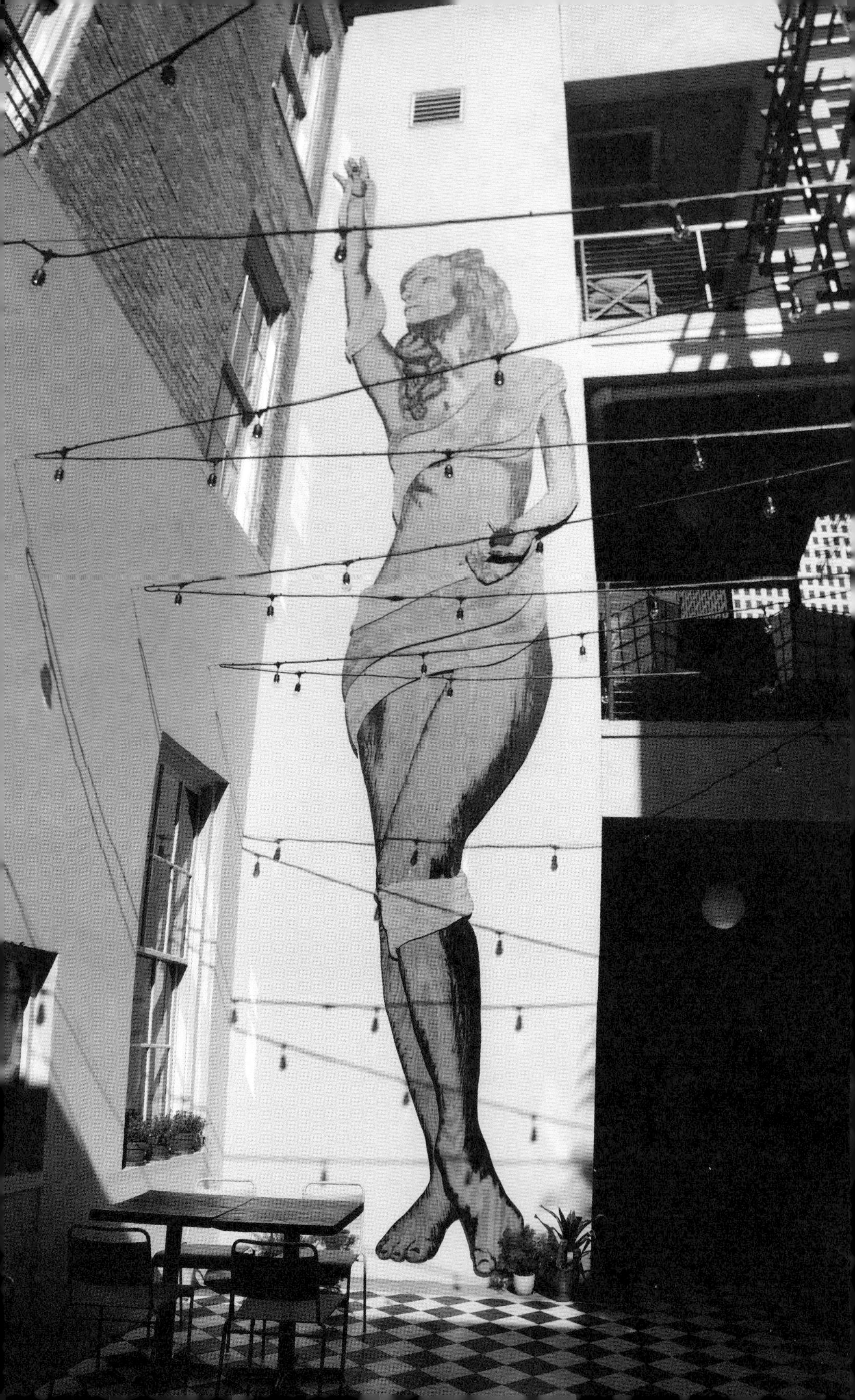

CONTENTS

INTRODUCTION

One of the most difficult parts of owning a tour company in New Orleans is all the stories that we never get to share with our guests. Sometimes we simply don't have enough time; other times the story's location is too far afield for your average tour. And finally, sometimes the secrets are just too strange for your average tourist. Tell a visitor that you can bathe in Napoleon's bathtub or visit part of the Eiffel Tower while in New Orleans, for example, and they may back away slowly. Explain that there's a religion in town that venerates the Grim Reaper or admit that your favorite bar sometimes has animals falling through the ceiling, and they're certain to run the opposite direction!

That is why we jumped at the chance to write this book. Inside you'll find some of our favorite New Orleans secrets, ranging from the truly obscure to local favorites that visitors often never hear. Because New Orleans is such a multicultural city, we wanted to present as many different stories as possible, with an emphasis on the often unheard and marginalized voices in our history. Inside are tales of enslaved peoples, immigrants, powerful women, and the LGBT community. There are also all the hallmarks of the Crescent City we love to tour and talk about: our cuisine, cocktails, jazz music, and even Voodoo can all be found within.

One more note: you may notice that the book is written in three different voices. One of us is a born-and-raised local; another is from "out in the country" of the Mississippi delta; and the third was a Midwesterner who—like so many visitors—fell in love with the city on a trip and never left! Because we all came to love the city in different ways, we wanted all of those relationships to be presented in this book, too. Once you are finished reading it, we hope you'll love New Orleans and her secrets as much as we do!

ABSINTHE MINDED

Where can one learn the truth about absinthe?

One of the most mysterious and misunderstood spirits is absinthe. A French—and therefore New Orleans—favorite, absinthe was said to cure a multitude of ailments and so it started as a medicine, as did most of today's liqueurs. While its inception was in Switzerland in the eighteenth century, absinthe peaked in popularity in nineteenth-century France. Artists and writers of the time appreciated its purportedly mind-opening effects and so it was drunk for more recreational reasons. Artists enjoyed watching the "Green Fairy's wings" as the sugar water dripped into the absinthe. While the spirit was banned in 1915 due to one of its ingredients being wormwood which contains thujone, a known hallucinogen, it continued to be available in New Orleans until 1940. It wasn't until 2007, when a serious investigation into the spirit was done by New Orleanian T. A. Breaux, that the ban was lifted. Because of this investigation and absinthe's immense popularity in New Orleans, its inclusion in the Museum of the American Cocktail was definitive. Today, absinthe fans can visit the museum to see the country's largest collection of absinthe artifacts, learn how it was (and is) made, and find out the truth behind its notorious reputation.

The French process of dripping sugar water into absinthe and the resulting white, milky liquid are called louche.

All the bottles behind this bar are various absinthes.

MUSEUM OF THE AMERICAN COCKTAIL

What: Largest absinthe collection

Where: In the Southern Food and Beverage Museum, located at 1504 Oretha Castle Haley Blvd.

Cost: $10.50 per person

Pro Tip: Once your education is complete at the museum, head over to Pirate's Alley Café next to the St. Louis Cathedral for a proper absinthe cocktail.

Southern Food and Beverage Museum on Oretha Castle Haley Boulevard.

ALL THAT JAZZ

Where can you watch the longest-running jazz band in the world?

In the city where jazz music was born, the Original Tuxedo Jazz Band is the oldest surviving jazz group. First organized in 1896 by Oscar "Papa" Celestin as the Tuxedo Jass Orchestra, the group moved into its namesake club, Tuxedo Dance Hall, in 1910. The club was located in the sixteen-block red-light district called Storyville, located just northwest of the French Quarter. Although it was spelled differently back then, most locals simply knew jazz as music "from the district." The club was shut down a few years later, but Celestin continued to lead the horns from the orchestra under the slightly revised title, Tuxedo Brass Band. Members included Louis Armstrong, Johnny St. Cyr, and other legendary musicians.

For over half of the band's 120-year history, some member of the French family has held the title of bandleader. Drummer and vocalist Gerald French has been in charge since 2011 when his uncle, Bob French, retired after thirty-four years at the helm. Bob had taken over from his father, Albert "Papa" French, making Gerald the third generation of the French

ORIGINAL TUXEDO JAZZ BAND

What: Dixieland jazz music in an old-school club

Where: Monday nights at the Royal Sonesta Hotel's Jazz Playhouse, 300 Bourbon St.

Cost: $$ (One-drink minimum per set)

Pro Tip: Since it is acoustic jazz, sit right up front! Pair it with dinner at the hotel's Restaurant R'evolution for a memorable night out.

The Original Tuxedo Jazz Band with bandleader Gerald "The Giant" French on the far right. Known for his unique, laid-back style of drumming and his smooth voice, French played for singers such as Charmaine Neville, the Dixie Cups, Dr. John, and Harry Connick, Jr.

family to lead "the Tuxedos," as the band is affectionately called.

The Tuxedo Jazz Band has played Dixieland jazz music for prime ministers, kings, and presidents (including Eisenhower's inauguration) and continues to tour a few times per year. Those in New Orleans can typically find them on Monday nights at the Royal Sonesta Hotel's Jazz Playhouse. Perhaps the swankiest jazz club in the city, patrons leave their cares behind the heavy velvet curtain at the door and instantly feel transported back to the first half of the twentieth century when jazz music was *the* sound.

The word "jazz" probably evolved from the mid-1800s slang word "jasm," which meant lively, energetic, vitality. It is first seen in writing to describe a California baseball pitcher's curve ball.

THE WINE BEHIND BARS

Why are there wine bottles behind bars on Royal Street?

Just one block from the debauchery of Bourbon Street is classy Royal Street. This street attracts people looking for antiques, jewelry, and amazing street music. However, there is one thing that most locals and tourists are likely to miss as they walk down the street. Located on Royal between St. Louis and Toulouse streets is what looks like a simple window with bars. People walking past don't often notice the barred opening with a few old wine bottles on display. But what's behind the bottles is a marvel! This is a window to the immense wine cellar at Antoine's Restaurant. A look beyond the bottles in the window unveils its true length, at 162 feet. It originally held 25,000 bottles, worth over two million dollars, which sadly was mostly lost during Hurricane Katrina. Today the collection has been restocked to include 18,000 bottles. The oldest bottle in the current collection dates back to 1811. This cellar, one of the largest in America, was installed around 1940 and stretches through various other buildings and over multiple lot lines. This fact, although not a big deal back in the 1940s, is currently causing issues between the city and the current owner, Mr. Rick Blount.

The owner, Mr. Rick Blount, allows spirit company owners and/or CEOs into the cellar to autograph their names next to the numbered box where their particular bottles are kept.

Viewing the wine cellar from Royal Street.

ANTOINE'S WINE CELLAR

What: Window to view Antoine's wine cellar

Where: Between 519 and 521 Royal St.

Cost: Free

Pro Tip: Bottles located within the first ten feet of the window are actually fake, as the heat and light near the window would spoil the wine.

A rare look inside the cellar. Spirits are arranged in numbered boxes along both walls of the cellar.

“BAYOU RABBIT?” NOPE

What is that weird creature you see by canals?

Nutria were originally prized for the lush layer of fur that lies beneath the scraggily outer hair. Brought from Argentina to Louisiana to establish a fur trade, famed Tabasco sauce founder E.A. McIlhenny is often blamed for the nutria problem after he turned them loose on Avery Island in 1941 to combat the water hyacinth, another invasive species. He denied sole responsibility and instead declared that he was the third nutria owner in the state, having bought his from a farm in New Orleans. A 1938 classified ad published in the *Times-Picayune* advertising “South American Swamp Beaver” for sale corroborates his story.

The real problem with nutria is their prolific reproduction. A female will have two to three litters every year with between five and seven babies in each. After just a few months, those babies are ready to start reproducing. What makes this rapid rate truly intolerable is the animal’s

---

Nutria are an invasive species that eat aquatic plants, roots, and small creatures that live in water (such as mussels and snails). Typically eating up to 25 percent of their body weight daily, their impact is exacerbated by their waste and damage to levees, structural foundations, and bank erosion due to their burrowing.

Nutria rodents (also called coypu) are perhaps best described as really, really large muskrats. Whereas a muskrat is merely 2 to 3 pounds full grown, the adult nutria is upward of fifteen pounds. Image by Herbert Aust from Pixabay.com.

NUTRIA

What: An unwanted critter

Where: Out the car window along any canal or marshy roadside

Cost: Free

Pro Tip: Despite the past attempt to get nutria on restaurant menus, there is nowhere in the New Orleans area to eat commercially prepared nutria. If you are looking to have a little fun, ask a butcher or grocery store manager if they sell nutria—you will likely get a rather animated response!

life span: the average nutria will live—and reproduce—for nine years! That reproduction rate is enough to make even rabbits blush.

Supplying enough food for this enormous population places a giant strain on the already endangered wetlands in coastal Louisiana. In 1997, conservationists and legislators secured a $2.07 million grant to entice people to hunt nutria (earning them $2 per tail) and throw them in a stew pot. With a flavor similar to rabbit, getting nutria on the menus would certainly help curtail the population. The problem lawmakers faced was convincing the general public to add nutria to their diets—it seems people were not keen to eat the “swamp rats” that they saw most often as roadkill. Today, about 300,000 nutria are hunted annually and yield $5 each.

BE NICE

Where can you get the original "Be Nice or Leave" art?

The phrase "Be Nice or Leave!" is sassy, bold, amusing, clever, and conveys an air of eccentricity. Not surprisingly, the man who made the saying popular embodies those same qualities, and his folk art store is every bit as interesting as one would expect.

Bob Shaffer became "Dr." Bob after he helped deliver his son via cesarean section. He had also been a forest ranger, construction worker, airplane builder, and more before relying on his self-taught art skills to pay the bills. Wood sculpture was his first medium until he ran out of suitable wood. Then he turned to paint, and his canvases were garbage can covers, folding chairs, plywood, and anything else he could find. Bottle caps adorn much of his art and add color, visual interest, and even nostalgia for old-time favorite brands.

He first saw the "Be Nice or Leave" phrase written in marker on a cardboard box at a Southern juke joint. He put it on a sign and hung it in his sculpture studio on Wilkinson Row in the French Quarter. It disappeared. He made another, and then another, but they all met the same fate.

Dr. Bob says his property once housed a shotgun house owned by Jean Lafitte (he still has the front of it) and later the Olympic Club Arena where Corbett defeated Sullivan in a 21-round boxing match that was the first heavyweight title fight in which participants wore gloves.

Dr. Bob's iconic art, complete with bottle cap border. When it comes to being a folk artist, Dr. Bob says it's about having soul, using real stuff, and always telling the truth.

The absolutely can't-miss sign outside Dr. Bob's door.

DR. BOB'S FOLK ART

What: Folk art store and studio

Where: 3027 Chartres St.

Cost: Free

Pro Tip: The sign says 10 a.m. to 5 p.m., 7 days a week, but as is true with *all* establishments in New Orleans, you may want to call ahead. When you do go, look for some of the great places in the area to stop for a bite or a drink, including Elizabeth's Restaurant, which has a nice collection of Dr. Bob's work adorning its walls.

Their constant disappearance clued Shaffer in that he was on to something.

Dr. Bob's Folk Art studio and shop is just downriver from the French Quarter in the Bywater neighborhood. It is the type of place that you instantly recognize when you see it. If the large, red dinosaur mailbox is not clue enough, then the rainbow-lit, giant arrow sign will do the trick. Once inside the gravel parking lot, more giant arrows direct guests to the shop. Dr. Bob has a very distinct style, often with a bayou alligator making a cameo. Artwork starts around $50.

BETTER THAN BEIGNETS?

Where can you get a sweet that helped enslaved women buy their freedom?

Despite having a much more interesting and important history than its cousin the beignet, the sweet rice fritters known as calas have all but disappeared from New Orleans.

When the Spanish took over the Louisiana colony in 1762, they introduced *coarteción*—the ability for enslaved people to buy their freedom from their owners. The enslaved had Sundays off, which provided the opportunity to congregate with other Africans for cultural and religious activities, rest, or to make and sell goods. With limited resources, many enslaved women took to selling street foods in the French Quarter to earn money. Rose Nicaud is famous for having bought her freedom by selling café au lait, eventually opening the first fresh coffee stand in the French Market. Another commodity the women sold were calas.

CALAS

What: A sweet treat with an important history

Where: Elizabeth's Restaurant, 601 Gallier St.

Cost: $$ (An order of calas is $5)

Pro Tip: An easy bike or cab ride from the French Quarter, Elizabeth's Restaurant is truly a New Orleans dining establishment. Walk off your satisfying meal by taking the Rainbow (shaped) Bridge at the base of Piety Street at Chartres to the Crescent City Park Trail and soak in beautiful views of the Mississippi River.

An order of "Old Fashioned Callas," as it is written on the menu, served with local product Steen's Cane Syrup for dipping.

The word *calas* (pronounced kuh-LAH) first appeared in writing in the 1880s. The name, like the treat itself, is believed to have been introduced by enslaved people who were trafficked from rice-producing regions of Africa. Calas are balls made of cooked rice, flour, sugar, and spices. They are deep fried and lightly dusted with powdered sugar and are typically served in the morning. *Coartecíón* was not allowed once the United States acquired the Louisiana Territory in 1803, but African women continued selling calas in the streets with the familiar cry, "Calas belles, calas tout chauds!" (Calas good, calas very hot!) until, by 1940, only a single calas vendor remained. They were made in African American homes for decades after, but now are nearly forgotten.

Fortunately, Elizabeth's Restaurant in the Bywater neighborhood continues to delight locals with this nostalgic treat. The restaurant is a destination on its own, with delicious, high-quality food at reasonable prices and the added bonus of funky New Orleans ambiance galore. It is especially popular for breakfast and brunch, but every item on the menu is going to be a winner.

Poppy Tooker, New Orleans food expert and host of *Louisiana Eats!* radio show on NPR, has been on a crusade to ensure future generations will know the history and recipe of this nearly forgotten dish.

BIB WORTHY

What is New Orleans BBQ shrimp, and how did it get named?

Here is what it *is not*: shrimp that has been smoked, grilled, or covered in a sticky, sweet vinegar-tomato sauce.

BBQ shrimp was an innovative recipe cooked up in an iconic New Orleans Italian restaurant in the 1950s. Frank Manale opened Manale's Restaurant in 1913 and ran it with his son and two nephews (Pascal and Jake). Upon Frank's death, nephew Pascal Radosta took over and eventually wanted his name on the sign while continuing to honor his uncle; thus, Pascal's Manale was born.

The oyster bar and the large, wooden beverage bar (a gift from Dixie Brewing Company in exchange for beer exclusivity at the restaurant) have both been with the restaurant since its opening. In 1954, BBQ shrimp completed the trio of special features. Pascal's friend raved about a shrimp dish he'd had in Chicago that used lots of butter and pepper. Pascal's attempt to recreate that dish was a failure, but what he came up with was even tastier! Pascal sautéed the large Gulf shrimp over high heat in a white wine, butter, Worcestershire, olive oil, and garlic sauce with cayenne pepper, black pepper, paprika, thyme,

---

Nearly 300,000 Italians (mostly from Sicily) immigrated to New Orleans between 1884 and 1924. To put this into perspective, the 1880 census showed just 216,090 residents in all of New Orleans!

Iconic Pascal's Manale Restaurant, still in the same family over 100 years later.

BBQ SHRIMP

What: A very messy but delicious sautéed Gulf shrimp dish.

Where: Pascal's Manale, 1838 Napoleon Ave.

Mr. B's Bistro, 201 Royal St.

Cost: $$$

Pro Tip: If you are given a bib, wear it! BBQ shrimp should be served with heads and tails still on, so be prepared to roll up your sleeves and get messy. Use the big piece of French bread to slather up the remaining sauce once the shrimp are gone.

oregano, and basil seasoning. It immediately went on the menu.

Pascal Radosta died in 1958 and was succeeded by his brother, Jake Radosta. Each of Pascal's children has run the restaurant at some point, and it remains with his youngest daughter's family today. Chef Mark DeFelice (Pascal's grandson) shed light on the naming peculiarity. He said that barbecue sauce, the sweet, tangy, tomato-based sauce, did not become popular in restaurants until the 1970s, so calling Pascal's creation a BBQ sauce was not confusing back then. This author believes it was the pepper and vinegar combination that qualified the recipe as yesteryear's classification of a BBQ sauce.

BLACKENING MOTHERSHIP

Where can you eat the original blackening seasoning?

Chef Paul Prudhomme comes from rural south-central Louisiana, which was settled by French-Catholic refugees who had been exiled from Acadiana (now Nova Scotia, Canada) in the late 1700s. As resourceful Cajun country folk, they ate whatever the land provided. This meant using herbs, spices, and slow-cooking methods to create hearty, flavorful meals.

The Cajun chef gained acclaim after moving to New Orleans and joining Ella Brennan at Commander's Palace in 1970. It was there that he had the idea of putting butter and seasoning on a piece of fish and placing it directly on a hot slab of iron, ultimately inventing a new style of cooking in the process: blackening.

He had created an instant sensation. The "junk" redfish—until then fit only for stew—became so sought-after for blackening that it was nearly fished out of existence until commercial fishing limits were put in place to ensure the species's survival.

Those tasting Chef Prudhomme's blackened redfish noted that it was much spicier food than they were used to. Being that he was the only Cajun chef with whom they had come into contact, people incorrectly attributed Cajun as always being spicy hot. Cajun food is consistently very flavorful, but it does not have to be spicy.

The late Chef Paul Prudhomme, left, was named Gene Autry Prudhomme in honor of his mother's favorite cowboy; the local priest added Paul to the birth certificate as his Christian name. Chef Paul Miller, K-Paul's executive chef since the mid-1990s, is on the right.

Prudhomme and his wife, Kay, used his newfound fame to open K-Paul's Louisiana Kitchen in 1980. He is credited as the first to fuse Creole and Cajun cuisines and for inventing (or at least popularizing) the Turducken recipe and tasso ham, which is like a Cajun prosciutto. Today, diners still make the pilgrimage to New Orleans to savor the original style of blackening at K-Paul's, which is much more balanced and less salty than other chefs have interpreted the dish. Prudhomme passed away in 2015, but Chef Paul Miller, his right-hand man since early Commander's Palace days, has been at the helm of K-Paul's since the mid-1990s, so the restaurant never skipped a beat. Miller and his wife of twenty years, Brenda (Paul Prudhomme's niece), keep their mentor's philosophy of "Good Cooking, Good Eating, Good Loving" alive with some of the freshest and most flavorful food in the country.

BLACKENED FOOD

What: A wonderful balance of seasonings and char flavor

Where: K-Paul's Louisiana Kitchen, 416 Chartres St.

Cost: $$$-$$$$

Pro Tip: Order the Surf & Turf. It is not on the menu, but you can ask for it: a piece of the blackened redfish along with a blackened filet mignon that is so tender a butter knife is all it takes! Another favorite is the Eggplant Pirogue with Seafood Atchafalaya. A pirogue is a flat-bottom Cajun canoe, but in this case, it is a deep-fried eggplant boat filled with fresh Gulf shrimp, bay scallops, crawfish, and sun-dried tomatoes in an herbed seafood sauce. Start with the gumbo (might be the best gumbo you'll ever eat) and save room for dessert!

HISTORY UNBOUND

Where can you learn about Free People of Color?

New Orleans had a prominent group of people of color who were not enslaved. Some earned money while they were slaves and bought their freedom. A larger number emigrated from Haiti and built homes, opened businesses, were highly educated, had money, and owned enslaved people themselves. Collectively, these people were known as "free people of color." They did not have all the same rights as white people, but they certainly were not enslaved. Free people of color made up 20 percent of the population in New Orleans and owned nearly a quarter of the French Quarter buildings in 1802.

That all changed in 1803. Once Louisiana became part of the United States via the Louisiana Purchase, free people of color lost their rights. They could no longer own property or walk through the city without papers documenting their lower-class status as "f.p.c." Determined to make a difference, this unique population in Louisiana made major contributions to the civil rights movement.

To tell their story, one local couple has opened Le Musée de f.p.c. in the Tremé neighborhood, which was the first suburb for African Americans in the country. The

---

Famous New Orleans Voodoo Queen Marie Laveau was a free person of color who was born around 1801 and died in 1881.

The outside of the museum on Esplanade.

FREE PEOPLE OF COLOR

What: Le Musée de f.p.c.

Where: 2336 Esplanade Ave.

Cost: $

Pro Tip: Call to make an appointment. Allow at least an hour and a half for the tour, but you might also wish to spend time reading the exhibits on your own and walking around the beautiful, tree-lined Esplanade Avenue.

Greek revival mansion on Esplanade Avenue bedecked with cast-iron decorative accents contains portraits, artifacts, furniture, inventions, artwork, and more that provide insight into the lives of these important people. Highlight artifacts include actual manumission papers granting a slave his freedom and the replica of a floor-to-ceiling petition that was signed by 1,000 free men of color urging President Lincoln to grant universal suffrage for black men, which prompted Lincoln to send a letter to Louisiana's governor on the topic. The real gem of the museum is the emotionally moving docent-led tour, which shares the compelling story of this unique community on a more personal and relatable level.

THE BEST GOOD MORNING COCKTAIL

Where might one find a bacon Bloody Mary made from scratch?

For Bloody Mary aficionados who believe that the key to a good Bloody Mary is in the mix and not in extravagant garnishes, Rampart Street in the French Quarter has something in store. On Saturday mornings, Bar Tonique, located at 820 North Rampart Street, has a house-crafted Bloody Mary that has locals and tourists in the know lining up.

The bartenders begin making their version of this tomato cocktail on Friday night by emptying a bottle of vodka into a large bowl and then frying bacon and pouring the fat into the vodka bowl. This mixture is covered and placed in the refrigerator overnight. The next day they remove the bowl, scoop out the solidified fat and pour the now bacon-infused vodka back into its original bottle. They then make their Bloody Mary mix by combining their own blend of spices with the juice of fresh tomatoes. It is said that a whole garden can be tasted in each sip. The mix is blended with the bacon-infused vodka, served over ice, and garnished with a strip of bacon. While it isn't the most

---

On Friday nights the bar exudes the aroma of cooking bacon while they prepare the vodka for the Saturday morning batch!

Bar Tonique's Bloody Mary garnished with a slice of bacon.

BACON BLOODY MARY

What: A bacon-infused Bloody Mary made with fresh vegetables

Where: Bar Tonique

Cost: $5

Pro Tip: Because all of their cocktails are made in-house from scratch with many ingredients, this is the place for serious cocktail aficionados to try well-crafted classics.

Bar Tonique, located on Rampart Street.

extravagant Bloody Mary ever, it is definitely one the tastiest. There's another reason why their Bloody Mary is so good: it only costs $5!

BOOZY CAKE

What is Russian Cake, and why did it start in Louisiana?

Russian Cake originated as a frugal way to utilize mismatched, stale pieces of cake, cookies, muffins, and pie crusts during the late 1800s. Sometimes called a Creole Trifle, pastry pieces were pressed into a smooth, rectangular box made of white pine with a removable lid and base. The layered scraps were "bound" together with alternating layers of fresh raspberry jelly before being generously doused with rum and a bit of anise flavoring. Heavy bags of flour rested on the box lid to compress the layers overnight. The ruby red cake was topped with white icing and tiny rainbow sprinkles.

Many theories exist as to the cake's beginnings. It is likely a combination of the raspberry trifle with the preparation style of punschtorte from Austria and Germany (where citrus punch and dark rum are poured in the cake's center) along with the idea of using a mold from the brandy-laced Charlotte à la Russe cake (translated as Russian-style charlotte). The "Russian" part of the name may stem from the latter, as some old family recipes call for wine instead of rum, but it likely was adapted from a popular tea found only in the southern United States called Russian tea. Invented around the same period as the cake,

---

When made properly, Russian Cake is flavorful, colorful, and exciting, with every bite just a bit different from the last.

A small piece of Russian Cake from Haydel's Bake Shop. The dense cake's taste is reminiscent of red licorice twists.

the drink was named after the Russian style of serving heated, ice-brewed tea with lemon and sugar. This simple tea recipe quickly evolved into any hot drink flavored with citrus and enhanced with rum (or sometimes wine) and spices.

Russian Cake is nearly extinct today, but it can still be found in New Orleans at Haydel's Bakery. This lavish cake continues to surprise visitors, delight children, and evoke nostalgia for adults. Interestingly, lamenters for this vanishing delicacy are found not only in Louisiana, but also in northeastern England! Bakers in England did not ice the cake, but otherwise, the recipe is nearly identical.

RUSSIAN CAKE

What: A dense, flavorful cake

Where: Haydel's Bakery: 4037 Jefferson Hwy.

Haydel's Bake Shop: 3117 Magazine St.

Cost: $

Pro Tip: Haydel's Bakery has Russian Cake at their bakeries and also online. Since they use rum extract instead of actual rum, eaters can consume it freely without worrying about its effects. Haydel's preparation and final presentation has not changed since the 1800; however, they no longer use scraps of stale pastries; today's version consists solely of a mix of leftover pieces of fresh or frozen cake. For an extra dose of uniquely New Orleans sweet treats, order a slice of the moisture-magnificent Doberge cake, too!

BOXING ON THE RIVER

Why is there a statue of two men fighting on the Mississippi River in Kenner, Louisiana?

Few people know that the very first official championship heavyweight boxing match was held in a suburb of New Orleans. The year was 1870 and bare-knuckled, no-holds-barred boxing was in danger of being outlawed for being barbaric, not to mention the gambling element it attracted. Kenner, Louisiana, a suburb about twelve miles from New Orleans, was chosen to hold the match, which took place on the bank of the Mississippi River in a section of Kenner that is today known as Rivertown. Kenner was chosen because it was as close as they could get to New Orleans without being harassed by officials intent on stopping the event.

Boxing matches in the late nineteenth century were often bare-knuckled bloodbaths that went on for an unspecified period of time. This event was no different. On May 10, 1870, "Gypsy" Jem Mace and Tom Allen—both English boxers—faced off in one round of bare-knuckled boxing that lasted forty-four minutes for a $2,500 prize, the equivalent of about $45,232 today. "Gypsy" Jem

---

Ironically, this first heavyweight bare-knuckle boxing match took place just a stone's throw up river from where the country's first *gloved* heavyweight boxing match took place in the Bywater neighborhood.

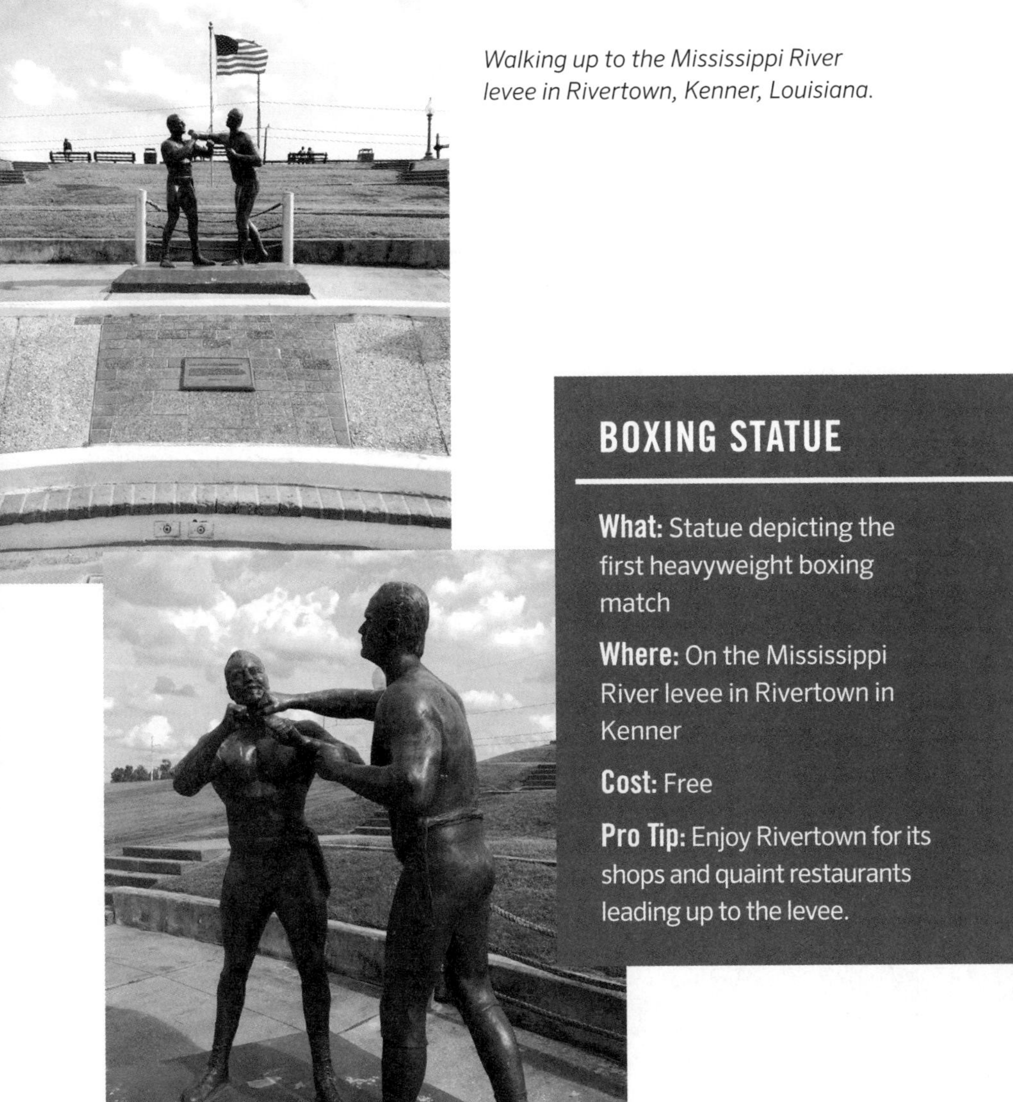

Walking up to the Mississippi River levee in Rivertown, Kenner, Louisiana.

The bare-knuckled fighters, mid-punch.

BOXING STATUE

What: Statue depicting the first heavyweight boxing match

Where: On the Mississippi River levee in Rivertown in Kenner

Cost: Free

Pro Tip: Enjoy Rivertown for its shops and quaint restaurants leading up to the levee.

Mace won the fight and retired thereafter. A bronze statue commemorates the event and can be seen on the levee in Rivertown.

KEEPING UP WITH THE STANTONS

How did jealousy and spite build one of the grandest houses in the Garden District?

Every homeowner has seen it happen: a house on the block gets a new fence, fountain, or swimming pool, and suddenly everyone seems to be updating their own homes to look just a little nicer than the neighbor's place.

Henry Sullivan Buckner took it a little further than most.

Buckner was a cotton kingpin living in New Orleans in the nineteenth century. When he had a falling out with his former business partner, Frederick Stanton, Henry decided to spite his former friend by hiring the famous architect Lewis E. Reynolds to design a new home for the Buckner family. Reynolds had already designed Stanton's Natchez, Mississippi, home, Belfast (now known as Stanton Hall), and Buckner gave the same architect only one mandate: whatever he built for Buckner needed to be bigger and grander than his rival's home.

Reynolds took Buckner's instructions to heart. Stanton Hall had been designed with two ballrooms, so the Buckner

BUCKNER'S MANSION

What: The Buckner Mansion, one of the largest properties in the Lower Garden District

Where: 1410 Jackson Ave.

Cost: Now closed to the public, the mansion can only be seen from the street

Pro Tip: While the set designer took cues from the real interior of the Buckner Mansion, the interior shots featured in *AHS: Coven* were actually shot on an 8,000 square foot soundstage.

At one time, the Buckner Mansion could be rented out as one of the largest short-term rentals in the city. The price tag? $4,800 a night!

Mansion would have three! Rather than several discrete porches and verandas, the Buckner home would have a single, wraparound porch that would encompass three sides of the home. Once finished, the mansion stood as the largest home in antebellum New Orleans, and even today, its approximately 20,000 square feet mark it as one of the largest houses in the already opulent neighborhood.

The mansion remained in the Buckner family until 1923, when it became the Soulé Business School (at one time considered the most prestigious business school in the South). Its sixty-year history as a school likely inspired its most famous incarnation: In 2013, the mansion was featured as "Miss Robichaux's Academy for Exceptional Young Ladies," the infamous (and thankfully fictional) school of witches in the hit series *American Horror Story: Coven*.

Top that, Frederick Stanton.

Both the mansion and the witches from *Coven* made a reappearance in the apocalyptic eighth season of *American Horror Story*.

A BAR THAT'LL MAKE YOUR HEAD SPIN

What is the most unusual bar in NOLA?

One of the most beautiful and beloved hotels in the French Quarter is the Monteleone. Opened in 1886 by Antonio Monteleone, the Hotel Monteleone is one of the last family-owned hotels in America. It is said that "the doorway to the French Quarter is through the lobby of the Monteleone."

The hotel itself isn't what attracts people from around the world: it's their bar. The Carousel Bar, located just off of the Monteleone lobby, is one of the most unique bars in America. Brought to the Monteleone in 1949, the bar is a true carousel that does a full revolution every fifteen minutes, pulled by a one-quarter horsepower motor. While a regular carousel has animals for the kids to ride, the Carousel Bar instead has chairs at the bar. Each has been hand-painted with animals that are so detailed, they appear to be stitched fabric instead of paint. While riding the carousel is fun, locals are more motivated by the very serious and well-respected cocktail program there. The

---

The bartenders need to be skilled not only at cocktail creation but also remembering which patron ordered which cocktail. Between the time the order is taken and when the cocktail gets delivered, the guests will have rotated to different places at the bar.

The Carousel Bar with its celebrated animal chairs.

Enjoying a cocktail with published author and bartender Marv Allen.

CAROUSEL BAR

What: A carousel-themed bar that actually rotates

Where: Inside the Hotel Monteleone, 214 Royal St.

Cost: $-$$ Depends on what is ordered

Pro Tip: Head to the gift shop and purchase the book *Magic in a Shaker* by Marv Allen. Then head back to the Carousel Bar and have Marv make you a cocktail while autographing your book!

Carousel Bar has been seen in various movies and has hosted a long list of famous writers, including Truman Capote and William Faulkner.

CULTIVATING A LEGACY

Where can you find the oldest oyster wholesaler in the country?

New Orleanians have had a long-standing love affair with our local mollusk. Roughly 50,000 Gulf oysters are eaten here every day! A large share of them are still cultivated and supplied by the first oyster wholesale company in the United States: P&J Oyster Company.

P&J Oyster Company opened in 1876 on Royal Street as Popich and Jurisich Oyster Company. It was a joint venture by the Jurisich brothers, Giuseppe (John, 23) and Giuseppe (Joseph, 21), and Antonio Popich (13). The trio traveled to the United States from Croatia/Dalmatia just a few years earlier to open an oyster farm at the mouth of the Mississippi River in Plaquemines Parish. Once established, the five sons of the Jurisich brothers were summoned to help grow the business.

And grow they did. P&J Oyster Company outgrew several French Quarter locations and eventually settled at 1039 Toulouse Street in 1921. This gave them easier access to the Basin Street Canal turnaround where many vessels unloaded their oysters.

That same year, a young banana import/export merchant, "Onofico" Alfred Sunseri, approached John

---

You can taste P&J's oysters at many area restaurants that proudly hold certification to serve them. The famous Oysters Rockefeller, invented in 1889 at Antoine's Restaurant, used P&J oysters.

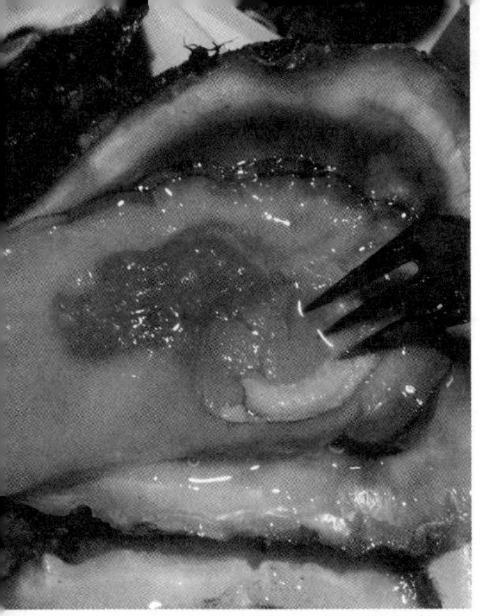

Restaurants proudly advertise their use of P&J oysters as a testament to their commitment of high-quality ingredients and fresh, locally sourced food items.

Jurisich about marrying his sister-in-law, Elvira. The Sunseri family had been nurturing relationships with merchants on the docks since their 1857 arrival from Trabia, Italy. Alfred's sales savvy and connections greatly contributed to P&J's growth, making it the largest oyster shipper in the south. He married Elvira in the early 1920s—and in doing so became cousin to the Jurisichs—and was made an equal partner in 1937.

Descendants of the three partners split the company's assets, and the Sunseri family remains the sole owner. Continuing the tradition built by their grandfather and father, brothers Al and Sal Sunseri oversee the operation today. Al's son, Blake, is prepared to carry on the legacy for the next generation.

P&J OYSTER COMPANY

What: Wholesale oyster distributor

Where: 1039 Toulouse St.

Cost: Free

Pro Tip: Oyster shucking is an early morning business, so the doors are often already closed by 10:30 a.m. There is no storefront or viewing area, but you can watch from the sidewalk at the entrance as oysters are unloaded by the fishermen, shucked, and then packaged and shipped out to area restaurants.

NOLA'S PERUVIAN CONNECTION

Where can one enjoy pisco in NOLA?

A short walk from the French Quarter, tucked away in the American Sector, is a boutique hotel with a most interesting bar. Located at 914 Union Street is the Catahoula Hotel, and in their lobby is a bar dedicated to the Peruvian brandy called pisco. Named appropriately enough, Piscobar offers a complete menu of the best pisco cocktails, such as the Pisco Sour, Pisco Punch, and the Chilcano, all made by bartenders who are clearly passionate about the spirit, its history, and how best to enjoy it.

The Catahoula Hotel is relatively new to the New Orleans scene, although the building dates back to 1845. The Catahoula Leopard Dog is the state dog of Louisiana, which is why there is the image of a dog's head in the hotel's logo. The courtyard just beyond the bar is a favorite place to enjoy a pisco cocktail under the oversized yet stylish mural of one of New Orleans's favorite burlesque dancers, Trixie Minx.

Exploring farther into the maze of rooms and floors, one can find the stairs to the rooftop bar. Here, one can enjoy the sun while sipping a cold Pisco Sour and mingling.

While people go for the pisco, it's also a great place for the vegans/vegetarians in the group.

The rooftop bar at the Catahoula Hotel.

PISCOBAR AT THE CATAHOULA HOTEL

What: Pisco in New Orleans

Where: Catahoula Hotel, 914 Union St.

Cost: $$ Average drink price is $12

Pro Tip: Look closely at the huge Trixie Minx mural (found on page iv). The "apple" she holds is actually a frying pan!

A Pisco Sour at the Piscobar.

ONE BIG PANCAKE

How did one pancake make a restaurant famous?

It's no secret that New Orleans has fantastic food. The focus of typical New Orleans dishes is flavor and/or complexity. Seldom is the focus on size or amount like, say, the Mt. Olympus burger at the Clinton Station Diner in New Jersey. "Seldom" is the key word here. For the late-night revelers looking for an after-party meal, there is one place with a dish that few would forget and fewer could finish.

Located just a few minutes outside of New Orleans in Metairie, Louisiana, is a small restaurant called City Diner. It's here that they serve a pancake that makes people reach for their smartphones in disbelief. The single pancake is the size of a pizza or a hubcap, and to tackle it is worthy of an episode of *Man V. Food*. This monster pancake can come plain or with your favorite fillings/toppings.

Around 2010, two cooks at City Diner were briskly handling their business in the kitchen when they knocked into each other, causing one to spill a large amount of batter onto the grill. Instead of cleaning it up and starting again they offered the huge pancake to the customer who proudly attempted to eat it. The rest is history, and today City Diner is THE place to go for those looking for a real culinary challenge.

While most people go to City Diner for breakfast, they also have some traditional New Orleans dishes, such as jambalaya and gumbo for lunch or dinner.

The huge pancake.

CITY DINER

What: One huge pancake

Where: 3116 South Interstate 10 Service Rd., Metairie

Cost: $6.49

Pro Tip: While they're famous for their huge pancake, their menu is equally large with some other great New Orleans dishes.

The pancake with a knife to really understand its size.

CIRCLES IN THE SQUARE

Why is the corner of a small city park so important to locals?

When French Louisiana adopted the Code Noir in the eighteenth century, it became illegal in New Orleans for an enslaved person to be required to work on Sundays. The French hoped that this law would help with the conversion of enslaved Africans to the Catholic faith and encourage assimilation into European culture. Though the enslaved gathered wherever they could (slaves were forbidden to assemble and so any gathering was always a dangerous affair), in 1817 the mayor of New Orleans restricted assembly to a specific section just outside of town that was informally called the *Place Congo*, or Congo Square.

Rather than causing the enslaved cultures to assimilate, this pair of laws had the opposite effect: varied ethnic groups (including the enslaved from Africa and the Caribbean, as well as several Native American tribes) set up a market, traded with one another, and shared aspects of their culture. Reveling in this once-a-week freedom, slaves sang, drummed, danced, and celebrated their native cultures, introducing

LA PLACE CONGO

What: Congo Square, a historic subsection of Armstrong Park

Where: Enter Armstrong Park at the corner of Saint Peter and North Rampart Sts.

Cost: Free

Pro Tip: Visit the area at 3 p.m. on Sunday for the best chance at witnessing a drum circle.

Mayor Latoya Cantrell had her inauguration celebration in Congo Square in 2018—a particularly powerful place to celebrate the first woman of color elected to the office.

Adewale Adenle's sculpture in Congo Square features djembe drums and a banjo (an instrument invented by slaves). Enslaved Native Americans are also represented (look for the woman with the braids), and the figure with scars on his cheeks is likely a Vodou priest.

the European community to the *congo* and *bamboula* dances. The rhythms echoing from the drum circles would eventually form the backbone of New Orleans's greatest cultural export, jazz music. And because these gatherings were often avoided by the European population (or only observed at a distance), Congo Square also provided cover for the enslaved peoples to practice their own religion: Voodoo.

Now part of Armstrong Park, the city voted in 2011 to restore the traditional name of Congo Square to that section. Evidence of Voodoo rituals can still sometimes be found at the base of the oak trees that encircle the Square, and though slavery has long been abolished, descendants of those cultures still gather on Sundays to celebrate their culture, heritage, and musical traditions.

The metallic circles that ring the interior of Congo Square were part of a water feature that was damaged during Hurricane Katrina. As of 2020, the fountain was still not operational.

STAND AND DELIVER

Where were the countless duels in New Orleans settled?

It could happen for almost any reason: political differences, a rivalry for a woman's affection, even a wayward glance or word. The result, though, was always the same—a slap of the glove across the face of the offender, and a challenge: meet at the Dueling Oaks at dawn to defend your honor or be forever branded a coward. As the sun rose over the bayou, gunshots would ring out, blades clashed and sparked, and honor would be restored—often at the cost of one (or more!) lives.

In the nineteenth century, more duels were fought in New Orleans than in any other American city, and most of those duels were fought under two matched oak trees called the Dueling Oaks. Pistols and swords were usually the weapons of choice, though records indicate bowie knives, sledgehammers, and even poison (with both men drawing lots to see who would consume the toxins first)! The duelists here weren't mere thugs or ruffians, either: the Oaks saw noblemen, United States congressmen, and even the president of the Louisiana Senate all draw steel under their shady boughs.

Jose Llulla, a famous duelist of the time, once purchased the Saint Vincent de Paul Cemetery. Rumors soon arose that there was a section of the cemetery "reserved" for the duelist's opponent-victims.

A Times-Democrat *article from 1892 reads, "Blood has been shed under the old cathedral aisles of nature. Between 1834 and 1844 scarcely a day passed without duels being fought at the Oaks. Why, it would not be strange if the very violets blossomed red of this soaked grass!"*

THE DUELING OAK

What: The site of the last duels fought in New Orleans

Where: 29591 Dreyfous Drive in City Park, where Dueling Oaks Drive meets Dreyfous Drive near the Besthoff Sculpture Garden and New Orleans Museum of Art

Cost: Free

Pro Tip: You can visit another popular dueling site, St. Anthony's Garden, in the French Quarter: the garden still stands directly behind St. Louis Cathedral.

Eventually, cooler heads prevailed, and laws against dueling began to be enforced in 1855. Paradoxically, that only encouraged further fighting under the Oaks—the police tended to only patrol areas near the heart of the city, while the Dueling Oaks were still conveniently on the outskirts of town. The last recorded duel under the Oaks took place in 1890, though some contend the tradition continued into the twentieth century.

Today, only one of the oaks still stands. No, the trees themselves didn't duel one another, despite lots of local jokes suggesting so—the missing oak was felled by a hurricane in 1949.

A PIECE OF PARIS IN NEW ORLEANS

How can you eat dinner in the Eiffel Tower while in New Orleans?

In 1981, city officials in Paris discovered a problem. The Eiffel Tower, Paris's most iconic landmark since its construction in 1889, was sagging. Engineers investigated the structure and determined that the Restaurant de la Tour Eiffel (added in 1937) was too heavy for the tower to support. They insisted that for the monument to survive, the restaurant needed to be removed. A Parisian businessman was the first to purchase the restaurant, only to learn that the city's administration would not let him reopen it anywhere in Paris under the Tour Eiffel name. Instead, he traded it to a New Yorker, who went searching for a buyer—and eventually found one in New Orleans.

The old restaurant was dismantled and shipped across the Atlantic Ocean in an enormous crate holding eleven thousand metal pieces. Once those pieces arrived in New Orleans, they were painstakingly reassembled on Saint Charles Avenue, and the restaurant that once sat more than five hundred feet above Paris found a new home

---

Technically speaking, the restaurant is the same one that once served historical figures like Pablo Picasso, Charlie Chaplin, and even Adolf Hitler...half a world away and hundreds of feet off the ground!

Eleven thousand pieces had to be reassembled to re-create the building on this side of the Atlantic. Makes you wonder if they had any leftover pieces when it was finished.

(albeit one a little closer to Earth—it now sits only sixteen feet above the ground!). In 1986, five years after its dismantling, the Restaurant de La Tour Eiffel officially reopened half a world away.

These days, the restaurant has metamorphosed into a special event venue and is one of the most popular Carnival parade-watching spots in the city. Now called the "Eiffel Society," it boasts an original chandelier of Edison light bulbs and has also added a "love lock gate," a wrought iron gate where lovers can attach a padlock (often with their names inscribed) and then throw away the key, mimicking yet another romantic Parisian custom.

THE EIFFEL SOCIETY

What: A venue and lounge built from the old Eiffel Tower Restaurant in Paris

Where: 2040 St. Charles Ave.

Cost: Varies by event, but guests can reserve a spot the week of Mardi Gras to watch the parades along Saint Charles Avenue for around $10.

Pro Tip: Didn't bring a lock? They sell them at the office for $15 ($20 engraved).

ENTER THE ZONE

Where can you find wood carvings that sing the blues?

Charles Gillam grew up in New Orleans's 9th Ward, but his current home in Algiers is where he is really making a difference. And his home is very easy to spot. The bright blue color is helpful, but the sculpture garden is the real giveaway.

Charles was already providing for himself at age sixteen by shining shoes in the French Quarter with his brother. Somewhat in awe of the artists he saw in Jackson Square, Charles asked one if he could have his discarded paint and brushes. He eagerly took them home and taught himself how to paint.

Throughout the next decades, his technique and media evolved. He started making sculptures with plaster and carving wood. His finished pieces are brightly colored and depict music and everyday life. Most are depictions of blues musicians made from driftwood retrieved from the Mississippi River bank, which lies directly across the street from his house.

Gillam became a full-time artist in 1994, in his early forties. It has been his goal since then to create an artistic environment where neighborhood children and young adults could feel safe expressing themselves through

---

Gillam says that the driftwood he finds whispers to him, and he just has to listen to hear who or what is inside that wood trying to get out.

Musical stairway mural across from Old Point Bar.

art, music, or even by playing basketball on the pavement nearby. This dream took a dramatic step forward in 2000 when Dr. Charles Smith, an Algiers native who had since moved to Illinois, was visiting family and heard how Gillam's work was impacting the neighborhood. Smith had been doing the same thing at his home near Chicago, and he inspired and mentored Gillam in his mission. The pair opened the Algiers Folk Art Zone & Blues Museum in Gillam's home that same year. Visitors can learn about local blues legends, see artistic renderings of New Orleans's second line parades and jazz funerals, and help support and preserve self-taught artists in the community.

ALGIERS FOLK ART ZONE & BLUES MUSEUM

What: A "living" folk art and blues museum celebrating self-taught artists.

Where: 207 LeBoeuf St. Viewings are by appointment only.

Cost: Donation

Pro Tip: Rent a bicycle and cross the river on the ferry. Bike the levee downriver to enjoy a gorgeous view of New Orleans all the way to the museum (it's easy to see from the levee). Grab a po-boy sandwich from River Fine Foods next door and picnic by the river while watching the giant cargo and cruise ships sail by. Stop at Old Point Bar for friendly conversation with locals and see Gillam's musical stairway mural before heading back to the ferry.

PRAYERS ANSWERED—SAME-DAY DELIVERY AVAILABLE

Who is the mysterious Saint "Expedite," and why do the locals venerate him?

It's a story almost too funny to be true.

In the early twentieth century, the clergy at the Our Lady of Guadalupe Church were excited to receive a new statue of Our Lady to adorn the vestry. When the statue arrived, the priests and nuns were puzzled by the inclusion of a second, smaller crate. Marked simply "EXPEDITE," it contained the statue of a Roman soldier holding a palm branch in one hand and a cross that read "Hodie" (Latin for "today") in the other. With no further explanation to be found, a smaller shrine was built to honor this strange inclusion, standing near the entrance of the church on the right-hand side. Understanding that the origin of the name was dubious at best, the church even included quotation marks on the nameplate: "St. Expedite."

This "too ridiculous to be true" story quickly took hold in the city's religious communities—both with the Catholics visiting the chapel and the Voodooists venerating

---

While many locals leave flowers and candles, Louisiana legend dictates that Saint Expedite's favorite offering is pound cake (specifically, Sara Lee store-bought pound cake). Who knew saints had such particular tastes?

Once called the Mortuary Chapel, Our Lady of Guadalupe originally served as a funeral chapel for victims of yellow fever epidemics. Back then, the church was dedicated to Saint Jude, patron saint of lost causes, which shows you the attitude New Orleanians had toward those who contracted the disease.

the tomb of their famous queen, Marie Laveau, in the neighboring cemetery. Legend holds among both groups that including a prayer at this particular shrine alongside other offerings (whether in the church or at Marie Laveau's tomb) will ensure that request is answered almost immediately—though perhaps not "today" as the saint's statue indicates. And according to the church, Saint Expedite is now considered the patron saint of emergencies, speedy solutions, and stands against procrastination.

We just wonder what would have happened if the crate had been marked "FRAGILE."

BLESSED SAINT EXPEDITE

What: A shrine to a confusing "Saint" honored by both Catholic and Voodoo practitioners

Where: Our Lady of Guadalupe Chapel, 411 North Rampart St. Saint Expedite can be found tucked into a corner on the right side of the church, between the glass entrance doors and the wall.

Cost: Free. The church is typically open until 5 p.m., but please be mindful and respectful of services and parishioners.

Pro Tip: Don't rush out like Saint Expedite! The church also has beautiful shrines to Saint Jude and Our Lady of Guadalupe, as well as an inspiring grotto outside dedicated to Our Lady of Lourdes.

THERE'S A STORM A-BREWING

How does a neon beer sign double as the city's most obvious weatherman?

On August 1, 1952, at precisely 8:00 p.m., the 126-foot-tall Falstaff Tower was lit for the very first time. Rising from the roof of the Falstaff brewery, ten-foot-tall letters vertically spelled out the name of the company, culminating in a large illuminated ball mounted twenty-one stories in the air. The sign could literally be seen from miles away, the logo dominating the central city skyscape.

The brewery was quick to point out, however, that the tower wasn't just the most obvious beer advertisement in the state. It also doubled as a weather forecaster for the metropolitan area. The color of the globe let the locals know what weather to expect: green for fair weather, red for cloudy, and white for showers. If the globe was flashing red, it meant rain; and if it was flashing red and white, storms were "brewing" (pun almost certainly intended).

The letters of the sign itself also acted as a temperature forecast. If the letters lit one at a time from the bottom up,

THE FALSTAFF TOWER

What: A twenty-one-story tower that forecasts tomorrow's weather

Where: Falstaff Apartments, 2600 Gravier St.

Cost: Free

Pro Tip: On the same building, you'll find a statue of a man holding a goblet aloft. He represents King Gambrinus, the unofficial "patron saint" of beer and brewing (even though he's not truly a Catholic saint!).

The man chosen to light the tower for the very first time was ninety-one-year-old Isaac Monroe Cline, a former local bureau chief of the National Weather Service.

temperatures were expected to rise. If the letters lit from top to bottom, temperatures were going to fall; and if the lights flashed on and off together, the temps were expected to stay constant. If you find all that difficult to remember, you weren't the only one! Falstaff took out an ad in the newspaper that included a preprinted key so locals could clip it out and carry it with them.

In December 1978, the brewery closed its doors and the tower went dark but remained a very visible landmark, even after Falstaff beer went out of production entirely in 2005. In 2011, the original metal letters were replaced with newer letters (designed to withstand 130 mph winds), and the tower was illuminated once more. Falstaff beer may be gone, but its largest advertisement still communicates tomorrow's weather—even today.

The National Weather Service's highest honor is called the Isaac M. Cline award, named for the same man who lit the tower for the first time in 1952.

THE WRITER IN THE ALLEY

Where can one buy a book in the home of a famous writer?

Many people don't realize how many famous writers have spent time in New Orleans over the years. Tennessee Williams, Truman Capote, Ernest Hemingway, and a host of others either lived in New Orleans or stayed long enough for bartenders to know their drink of choice. One celebrated writer who called New Orleans home was William Faulkner. In 1924, Faulkner came to visit his friend Sherwood Anderson, who lived in the French Quarter. After staying with Anderson for a while, Faulkner's desire to stay and write led to his finding his own place nearby: Pirate's Alley to be exact. In this apartment, Faulkner wrote his first published novel titled *A Soldier's Pay*. After Faulkner moved on from New Orleans, the building fell into disrepair. Years later, Ms. Rosemary James and Joe DeSalvo purchased the building and restored it to its former glory. They appreciated its history as Faulkner's living quarters and so decided to open a bookstore on the first floor. Faulkner House Books is a beacon for literature fans who enjoy the thought of buying books in a place where Faulkner lived and wrote. Those wishing to pay a visit need only to find Jackson Square and then walk into

---

In 1958, Elvis Presley ran down this very alley in the movie *King Creole*.

Faulkner House Books in Pirate's Alley.

FAULKNER HOUSE BOOKS

What: Where Faulkner stayed in NOLA

Where: 624 Pirate's Alley

Cost: Free

Pro Tip: Stop in at the Pirate's Alley Café for a favorite drink of Faulkner's: Absinthe.

William Faulkner's small room was just inside the door to the right. Ask the person working there to point it out.

the alley to the left of St. Louis Cathedral. This is Pirate's Alley. Faulkner House Books is next door to the Pirate's Alley Café.

FIT FOR A...COUNT?

Where can you see French Quarter eccentricity at its finest?

Arnaud Cazenave adored the finer things in life. A wine salesman from France, he opened his namesake Arnaud's Restaurant in 1918 where patrons enjoyed the luxurious atmosphere as much as the French-Creole food and drink. Arnaud loved making a stately entrance there and at any lavish social affair, enchanting others with a personality as kaleidoscopic as his attire. It was his charisma and exuberance that earned him the honorary (and perhaps self-proclaimed) title: Count Arnaud.

His daughter, Germaine, likewise yearned for the spotlight everywhere she went. Her public relations efforts landed Arnaud's as "Paris of the South" in newspapers from New York to France. She inherited the restaurant in 1948, along with her father's magnetism, flamboyancy, and penchant for scandal. She also earned the title of queen; between 1937 and 1968, Germaine reigned as queen over twenty-two Mardi Gras balls, more than any other woman in Carnival history.

Forever the eccentric, Germaine selected Archie Casbarian to take over the restaurant in 1978 due to the many resemblances he held to her father, including his initials. However, the Casbarians turned out to be a

---

The restaurant is a labyrinth comprised of 11 buildings patched together over a 30-year span to create 14 private dining rooms in addition to the main dining spaces.

The museum has several life-size mannequins that look alike and are slightly damaged with age, giving the museum a somewhat eerie feeling. Each wears an elaborate Mardi Gras gown and jewels.

good choice because they resurrected the deteriorating restaurant to its original glory, careful to retain as many original elements as possible. This included the chandeliers, china patterns, cypress paneling, and iconic Italian floor.

While the restaurant contains a century's worth of secrets, the most opulent is hidden above the bar. A tiny entrance, just to the left of the main reception desk, leads to the Germaine Cazenave Wells Mardi Gras Museum. It opened in 1983 and holds a treasure trove of gowns, masks, costume jewelry, photographs, and other memorabilia of Carnivals past, all part of the colorful Cazenave estate. In good New Orleans fashion, the display is as equally beautiful as it is creepy, since one cannot help but feel the Count's and Queen's presence in the unusual space.

GERMAINE CAZENAVE WELLS MARDI GRAS MUSEUM

What: A collection of Mardi Gras gowns and memorabelia

Where: Arnaud's Restaurant, 813 Bienville St.

Cost: Free

Pro Tip: The museum is open during regular restaurant hours. Be sure to stop by the James Beard award-winning Arnaud's French 75 Bar for a libation during your visit, preferably before heading upstairs to the museum. Not only are their cocktails something to remember, but the museum viewing seems to have more of an impact when one is in a more "spirited" mindset.

FIT FOR A KING

How did a teenage boy invent a potato dish for the King of France?

Reared in France, young Antoine Alciatore spent long hours at the farmers market learning about exotic spices and produce. His father, a tailor, bragged about his son's culinary interest to his client, notable French chef Collinet. The chef was impressed with the eight-year-old boy and took him on as an apprentice.

Chef Collinet was asked to orchestrate a lavish meal for King Louis-Phillip to commemorate a new railroad connecting Paris with Saint Germain-en-Laye. The region's top chefs were involved, and Antoine, Chef Collinet's star pupil, was put in charge of the potatoes, which the king preferred fried. A large cauldron of oil was set over a fire outside. When the train arrived, Antoine carefully placed his strips of potato into the oil.

A messenger appeared halfway through the cooking process to announce that the king was delayed, having followed the train in a chariot since safety on the untested railway was a concern. Antoine immediately ordered his helpers to pull the potatoes from the pot. Surely, they were ruined, as was Antoine's chance to impress. He kept himself occupied by weaving baskets from the potato peels until finally, the king arrived.

Born in Italy as Angelo Alciatore, Chef Collinet remarked that any French cuisine apprentice of his needed a French name, so he called him Antoine.

Soufflé potatoes with a side of béarnaise sauce for dipping.

The potatoes were loaded back into the oil. To Antoine's surprise, they puffed up and filled with air! The oil had become hotter during the wait and caused this peculiarity. He nervously placed the puffed strips into the baskets, and they were whisked off to the king.

King Louis-Phillip enjoyed them so much that he chastised Chef Collinet for keeping the dish secret. The chef assured the king that his apprentice, Antoine, had only recently invented the dish. The king summoned Antoine, who at just fifteen years old, feared his future was ruined. Instead, the king commended him and demanded to know the name of this inventive potato. Being put on the spot by the King of France, Antoine announced: "Soufflé potatoes" with wide eyes, to which the king nodded approvingly.

SOUFFLÉ POTATOES

What: Not-your-average fried potato

Where: Antoine's Restaurant, 713 St. Louis St.

Cost: $$$-$$$$ ($8 for the Pommes de Terre Soufflées (potatoes), which can also be ordered at Antoine's Hermes Bar)

Pro Tip: Arrive thirty minutes before meal service begins and ask for a tour of the back dining rooms. They are beautifully decorated, full of collectibles, and will give you an insider's view of the Mardi Gras festivities and traditions that are not shown on television.

HOME IS WHERE THE HEART BREAKS

Where can you see the aftermath of Hurricane Katrina as if it were yesterday?

On the morning of August 29, 2005, Hurricane Katrina roared into the Gulf Coast region, making landfall just east of New Orleans. At around 9:30 a.m., two thirty-foot-long sections of the London Street Canal Levee, straining against the pressure of the ensuing storm surge, suddenly collapsed. As a torrent of water poured through the gap, the Gentilly neighborhood was immediately and irrevocably changed. Hundreds of people died as a consequence of the breach, and as many homes throughout the neighborhood were destroyed.

Those residents who survived counted themselves lucky, but upon coming home found only more tragedy. The few homes that weren't destroyed entirely were infested with rot, black mold, and the grime of sitting untouched for months in the heat and humidity of Louisiana. Furniture was broken and scattered, having floated to the ceiling only to return in strange formations once the water receded.

One of the most dramatic pieces in the display is the battered newspaper that reads "KATRINA TAKES AIM." That's the actual front page of the *Times-Picayune* from August 28, 2005.

It's hard to imagine now, but Warrington Drive used to be lined with houses and shaded with huge oak trees. Today, the only trees that exist were planted post-2005. You can see some images of the neighborhood as it was on the brick columns of the house.

More than a decade after the storm, at the site of that breach, evidence of the devastation remains: empty foundations where homes once stood, weed-choked lots that were once shaded by oak trees, and a single house where the devastation has been painstakingly and heartbreakingly recreated by levees.org (a local environmental group). Created by Aaron Angelo, a mixed-media artist, and Ken Conner, a theatrical set designer, the Flooded House Museum was built inside one of the surviving homes and "furnished" with artificial mold, rot, and even furniture just as it would have been seen in the storm's aftermath. Located just yards from the fateful breach, the museum now stands as a life-sized diorama of the devastation perpetrated by Hurricane Katrina and a sobering reminder of the day in New Orleans that everyone's life was literally turned upside down.

THE FLOODED HOUSE MUSEUM

What: A life-size replica of a house that suffered flooding from Hurricane Katrina

Where: 4918 Warrington Dr., off Mirabeau Ave. in the Gentilly neighborhood

Cost: Free and open to the public from dawn to dusk

Pro Tip: Eagle-eyed viewers may be able to spot the exact site behind the museum where the levee breached—the new section is a different color and texture than the older walls.

THE "GATEWAY" OYSTER

What oyster is so delicious that even non-oyster eaters love it?

Many of the 50,000 oysters eaten daily in New Orleans are fried and served on platters or in po-boy sandwiches, and a large percentage are consumed raw. However, there is a third style that locals and visitors alike devour with reckless abandon: the charbroiled oyster.

The history of the charbroiled oyster started in 1969 when Drago and Klara Cvitanovich opened Drago's Restaurant in the Fat City neighborhood. Originally from Yugoslavia, the two met in the 1940s while each was visiting New Orleans during Mardi Gras. They fell in love and were married three weeks later. Their son, Tommy, has been in the restaurant business virtually since birth and is the second generation to run Drago's.

DRAGO'S SEAFOOD RESTAURANT

What: Charbroiled oysters

Where: 3232 N. Arnoult Rd.

1 Poydras St. (inside the Hilton Riverside Hotel)

Cost: $$

Pro Tip: Chew carefully! Many diners find pearls in the oysters. They are small, but still very hard. If there is no room at the Hilton location's char bar and you are not looking to have a full meal, grab a seat in the hotel's lounge adjacent to the restaurant for faster service and walk over to the char bar to watch the process for a few minutes.

Drago's charbroiled oysters, hot off the grill.

It was Tommy who changed the course of oyster history forever. One day in 1993, he took his father's popular grilled redfish recipe and said, "I wonder how this would taste using an oyster?" And the charbroiled oyster was born.

The dish consists of a shucked, local Gulf oyster in the half-shell that is placed directly onto a flame grill. Restaurant recipes vary slightly, but the basic premise is to slather the oyster with garlic butter, herbs, and parmesan cheese. Once it is grilled to perfection, the oysters are placed on a platter and served with a chunk of New Orleans French bread, which is used to soak up the extra butter and cheese once the delectable oyster is eaten.

Tommy's invention appears to be the first time that an oyster was heated from the bottom up and served commercially. Many restaurants have since copied the dish, which is also referred to as a chargrilled oyster, but only Drago's has a char bar with specially designed oyster grills. Eaters can feel the heat emitted by the four-foot-high flames and watch with hungry anticipation as their seafood treats sizzle.

Gulf oysters are unique in that they receive minerals and nutrients from both fresh water and salt water, which is why they tend to be large with some sweetness, some salinity, and very heavy, thick shells.

GONDOLA WITH THE WINDS

How did a Venetian gondola survive two hurricanes to end up in New Orleans?

Gondolier Robert Dula (or "Roberteaux," as he's often called) was introduced to gondolas by a rather interesting character: James Bond (in the movie *Moonraker*). "When I saw James Bond zipping through the canals of Venice in a high-performance gondola, I told my mom, 'I'm gonna get one just like James Bond.'"

The twists and turns that led to the realization of Robert's childhood dream rival those of any spy adventure. An online correspondence with a Venetian boat builder led to a virtual introduction to Joseph Gibbons, who operated a gondola business in Boston and invited Robert to head north to train as a proper gondolier. In 2003, Robert commissioned his own gondola to be built in Venice, christening it the *Bella Mae* after his mother.

Unfortunately, once the *Bella Mae* arrived in the United States, trouble seemed to follow close behind. The boat arrived in Pensacola, Florida, in 2004, only for Robert's fledgling business to be swept away by Hurricane Ivan. Robert saved the *Bella Mae* by sinking her in a local

---

In 2019, the adjacent Besthoff sculpture garden doubled in size and now contains more than ninety sculptures from mostly modern artists, many of which can be admired without leaving the comfort of the gondola cruise!

Roberteaux takes the Bella Mae *and two passengers under the bridge separating the "Big Lake" from the Besthoff Sculpture Garden.*

waterway, and after retrieving and cleaning the boat, decided to start over—this time in New Orleans. Hurricane Katrina would hit five months later. Again, Robert sank his beloved gondola to save her, but because of Katrina's lingering effects, this time the gondola remained submerged for over a month before she was able to be retrieved and repaired.

These days, both Robert and the *Bella Mae* are at home in City Park, sharing a dock with the park's paddleboats and offering rides through the Besthoff sculpture gardens, the "Big Lake" of the park, and several smaller waterways. The *Bella Mae* is as unique as she is resilient: she's the only Venetian gondola in Louisiana, and one of only two dozen in the entire United States.

THE NOLA GONDOLA

What: An authentic Venetian gondola offering excursions Wednesday through Sunday from 4 to 7 p.m.

Where: Big Lake Trail in New Orleans City Park, very near the New Orleans Museum of Art

Cost: $100 for a fifty-minute cruise for two people, $10/ person for extra passengers (up to six). Advance reservations required at nolagondola.com.

Pro Tip: Make sure to pick up a bottle of champagne or prosecco ahead of time for a true Italian experience. Roberteaux will provide the glasses, ice bucket, ice, and corkscrew!

GRASSHOPPERS FOR BRUNCH?

Where would having a Grasshopper cocktail for brunch be a lesson in history?

Many eating and drinking establishments in New Orleans are known for either a signature culinary or cocktail invention. One old restaurant in the French Quarter has the rare distinction of two! Tujague's Restaurant, located on the corner of Madison and Decatur, has been there since 1856, and while they are famous for a Creole brisket, it's their brunch and Grasshopper cocktail that will put Tujague's in the history books.

Tujague's was originally a few doors down from their current location. What was in the current location was a restaurant called Begue's Exchange. "Madame Begue" was famous for her 11:00 a.m. breakfast, which was often very long and offered alcoholic beverages. Because she had a small dining room, she offered to send the overflow a few doors down to Tujague's. This meal became known as the "Butcher's Breakfast," as it was offered at a convenient time for third-shift workers who were typically butchers from the French Market. This concept took off, first with locals and then with visitors who were in New Orleans for the Cotton Centennial in 1884—also known as the first World's Fair. The meal's name was later shortened to

---

When dining at Tujague's, be sure to try their famous Creole brisket.

Left: Tujague's Restaurant on Decatur Street. Right: The Grasshopper cocktail.

GRASSHOPPERS AT TUJAGUE'S RESTAURANT

What: Brunch and the Grasshopper cocktail

Where: 823 Decatur St.

Cost: Grasshopper: $10
Brunch: $$

Pro Tip: Notice the bar. It was already ninety years old when it was brought over from France in 1856.

"brunch," which of course is the combination of the words *breakfast* and *lunch*. Eventually Madame Begue retired and Tujague's took over her location in 1910 and continued offering brunch in the space where it all started.

Brunch in New Orleans is typically a boozy meal served a bit later than the normal breakfast time. "Boozy" is the key word here, and Tujague's has that covered as well.

In the early 1900s, Philibert Guichet, the owner of Tujague's at the time, mixed together cream, crème de menthe, crème de cocoa, and a topper of Brandy to create the minty Grasshopper cocktail. It was a hit and even won a cocktail contest in New York. The cocktail has gone around the world, and in some places (read: Wisconsin) they make the cocktail with ice cream!

THE GUMBO SHOP'S MURAL

Where can you see what Jackson Square looked like in the eighteenth century?

Jackson Square is the center of the French Quarter and everything radiates from it. French, Spanish, and American history can be observed here all while appreciating a horn band and wolfing down some beignets. But the way it looks today is very different from what the square looked like in the 1700s.

Since this era in history predates photography, we can only rely on a few drawings to give us an idea of what the square looked like back then. One drawing in particular shows the square in detail and is large enough to cover one wall of a restaurant. From this rendering, we know that before the square was named for Andrew Jackson, it was called the Place D'Arms. It was a parade ground for the French and later in 1762 for the Spanish armies (as the Plaza de Armas). This was where military parades and even hangings took place.

The source of this information comes from a restaurant. The Gumbo Shop, located just steps from Jackson Square, gives its diners the chance to see what Jackson Square looked like in the late eighteenth and early nineteenth centuries. Sadly, most people don't even notice it! Patrons

---

When dining at the Gumbo Shop, be sure to get one of their delicious fresh fruit daiquiris.

Gumbo Shop mural of the Place D'Arms. Notice the clothing and how different the Cathedral looked. Go to page 3 to see the mural on the adjoining wall, which is the perspective looking at Decatur Street in front of the Place D'Arms.

THE GUMBO SHOP

What: The mural in the dining room at the Gumbo Shop

Where: 630 St. Peter St.

Cost: $$

Pro Tip: Observe the mural while enjoying the Gumbo Shop's combination platter: red beans & rice, shrimp creole, and jambalaya. For an extra buck you can upgrade the red beans & rice to crawfish étouffée.

need only look at the wall adjacent to the door through which they just entered to see the mural. Of particular interest are the architecture of the St. Louis Cathedral and the clothing of the bystanders watching what seems to be a military display. Few antique pictures bring the observer into the moment quite as well as this one does.

THE MOTHER OF THE HOLY FAMILY

Will a humble New Orleanian become the first African American Catholic saint?

"I believe in God, I hope in God. I love. I want to live and die for God."

These were the words that Henriette DeLille, a free woman of color, wrote after having an intense religious vision. In 1836, at the age of twenty-four, she abandoned a life of privilege and dedicated herself to working with the poor, needy, and enslaved. She petitioned the Catholic Church to become a nun but was rejected: the Ursuline and Carmelite orders were open only to whites.

Undeterred, Henriette founded a home that cared for elderly nonwhites and taught religion and literacy to both free people of color and slaves—despite the fact that educating nonwhites was illegal in Louisiana. That home became the Convent of the Holy Family, the first convent in the United States for black women. In 1852, fifteen years after her vision, Henriette officially took her vows and became the order's Mother Superior. When she died in 1862, her obituary would read "for the love of Jesus Christ, she had become the humble and devout servant of the slaves."

In 2001, the Lifetime television network released a movie called *The Courage to Love*, with Vanessa Williams portraying Mother Henriette.

Mother Henriette became a controversial figure once again when records uncovered that she may have had two children out of wedlock before her religious epiphany. While conservative Catholics argued this disqualified her from sainthood, both her biographer and the archdiocesan archivist pointed out that this happened before her confirmation, and the Church has continued to move forward with her process.

But Henriette's story would continue long after her death. In the late 1960s, modern Sisters of the Holy Family approached the archbishop of New Orleans about beginning Henriette DeLille's canonization (the process of becoming a saint). The archbishop's response: "What took you so long?"

There are officially four phases in the canonization process: In 1988, she was declared a Servant of God (step 1); and in 2010, Pope Benedict declared her Venerable (step 2). The city now awaits confirmation of two miracles. If confirmed, Henriette DeLille would become the first true New Orleans saint (the NFL notwithstanding) as well as the first African American saint in the Catholic faith.

And we'll be sure to ask the Church: What took you so long?

VENERABLE MOTHER HENRIETTE DELILLE

What: A historic woman poised to become America's first African American Catholic saint

Where: A plaque commemorating Henriette DeLille can be found at the intersection of Royal and Orleans Sts. in the French Quarter; the Bourbon Orleans hotel nearby stands on the site of the original convent

Cost: Free

Pro Tip: If you'd like to pay your respects, Mother Henriette is interred in Saint Louis Cemetery #2, alongside dozens of members of her order. The modern Sisters of the Holy Family can be found at their Motherhouse, 6901 Chef Menteur Highway or at sistersoftheholyfamily.com.

EUREKA! THE WAR IS WON!

How did one New Orleans businessman single-handedly contribute to winning World War II for the Allies?

Andrew Higgins built his first boat in a basement at twelve years of age. It was apparently so large that a wall had to be demolished to remove the craft. Just like that, Higgins's lifelong love affair with boat building began.

By the 1930s, Higgins was established in Louisiana's lumber and oil industries. He had already designed a boat to navigate the shallows where loggers and drillers often ran aground while exploring. With a propeller protected by a recessed tunnel, the boat could traverse the shallower waters and even be beached and relaunched with ease. Higgins dubbed his invention the Eureka boat, and for several years his small shipbuilding company produced a handful locally.

Then the United States military came calling.

They were looking for a craft that would let them land

THE EUREKA BOAT

What: The "Higgins Boat" which won the Battle of Normandy during WWII

Where: The National WWII Museum on (where else?) Andrew Higgins Blvd. between Magazine and Camp Sts.

Cost: The museum is open daily 9 a.m–5 p.m. Tickets are $28/adults, $18/students and military, and free for WWII veterans.

Pro Tip: While the Higgins Boat that sits in the museum's main building is a replica, you can see an actual historic Higgins Boat in the museum's Restoration Pavilion!

Technically, the replica boat can be seen in the box office without even buying an admission to the museum, but we wouldn't recommend it. A full exhibit surrounds the boat with artifacts, videos, and occasionally even one of the Higgins Boat builders is available to answer questions!

on unguarded beaches in order to avoid detection and attack, and Higgins's design fit the bill. The contract changed both Higgins's career and the US Navy. In 1938, Higgins employed seventy-five workers; by 1943, he was employing around 25,000. Similarly, by 1943 fully 92 percent of the ships in the United States Navy had been designed by Higgins Industries!

On June 6, 1944, the Eureka boat (renamed the Higgins Boat) would help transport tens of thousands of troops onto the beaches of Normandy. Leaders from both sides recognized Higgins's contribution: Eisenhower would call Higgins "the man who won the war for us," while Hitler angrily complained of "the new Noah" who had made D-Day possible.

Higgins died in 1952 without much fanfare, but his legacy lives on. The National D-Day Museum (originally constructed in New Orleans because of the Higgins connection) has grown into the National World War II Museum. Its first exhibit? A brand-new Higgins Boat, built to WWII specifications by more than one hundred surviving Higgins Industries workers.

Andrew Jackson Higgins was probably as famous for his bombastic personality as he was for his shipbuilding skills. Family members fondly recalled his love of bourbon and the magic tricks he would perform for the Higgins children.

A TRUE NEW ORLEANS ARTIST

Who painted the mural of New Orleans on the side of the Hilton Riverside?

Located on the side of the Hilton Riverside hotel is a huge mural of New Orleans. Although thousands of people enjoy the mural on their travels up and down Convention Center Boulevard, few know the man behind the art. One of the most prolific and respected artists in New Orleans today is Terrance Osborne. Osborne was born in 1975 in the country's oldest African American neighborhood: the Tremé (pronounced: truh-MAY).

When he was sixteen, he started painting in a style so unique that by the time he was in college he was discovered and quickly became the sensation he is today. Terrance's art portrays life in New Orleans from crawfish boils and street flooding to Mardi Gras parades and his own dog. His use of vibrant color reminds one of New Orleans's Caribbean background. One way to know that one is looking at an original Osborne is to examine the medium closely. He doesn't paint on canvas. Instead Osborne paints on large sheets of plywood. Wood is much cheaper than canvas, which was important for a college kid's budget.

After viewing the Osborne mural, walk a few feet down Convention Center Blvd. to see the Wyland mural in the parking lot of the Riverwalk Mall.

Mural on the side of the Hilton Riverside on Convention Center Blvd.

HILTON HOTEL MURAL

What: Mural on the Hilton Riverside

Where: #2 Poydras St. and the Terrance Osborne Gallery: 3029 Magazine St.

Cost: Free

Pro Tip: Pictures are allowed using your cell phone but not high-end cameras. Notice how all of your senses are tapped during your visit.

Each year the Jazz and Heritage Festival chooses one artist for their famed Jazz Fest poster. Being chosen is a huge honor, as it is one of the highest grossing festival posters in the world. Terrance has been chosen five times!

Today he gets commissioned by the likes of Hilton, Heineken beer, Coca-Cola, Subway, and Harrah's Casino, to name just a few. His art is taught in universities, and people have even tattooed reproductions of his art on their bodies! Osborne's art gallery was voted best art gallery in New Orleans after being open only six months. Visiting his gallery located at 3029 Magazine Street is a breathtaking experience not to be missed by those enjoying the Garden District.

HOLLYWOOD SOUTH

Where can you visit the site of the world's first movie theater?

It seems only fitting that the same city that housed the first opera house in the country should also be home to the first movie theater. But Canal Street's Vitascope Hall, opened July 26, 1896, was not only the first theater in the country, it was actually the first for-profit movie theater in the entire world.

Businessman William T. Rock licensed one of the very first moving-picture projectors and set up shop at 623 Canal Street. From 10 a.m. to 3 p.m. and 6 p.m. to 10 p.m. daily, patrons could step into the showhouse and watch a thirty-second movie for ten cents. The pictures comprised ordinary activities strung together into a montage. A few seconds of Niagara Falls followed by a posing muscle man changed to a woman feeding pigeons and then to a toboggan run clip. It was as if a slide show had been put together in a way that allowed each photograph to come to life for a few seconds before switching to the next image. Those who were extra enchanted with the technological breakthrough of capturing motion on film could pay an

---

"Pop" Rock, as he was known, first showed the movies as a temporary exhibit. It was met with such immense success that just one month later he and business partner Walter Wainwright opened the permanent Vitascope Hall theater.

Top: An image published in 1916 in the industry publication The Motion Picture News *shows Vitascope Hall. (National Archives) Bottom: VooDoo Mart now resides in the former Vitascope Hall.*

VITASCOPE HALL

What: New Orleans's first movie theater

Where: 623 Canal St.

Cost: Free

Pro Tip: New Orleans retains very close ties with the film industry. So many television shows and movies are filmed in the city that it is known as Hollywood South. If you see signs posted along the street that show odd words in all-capital letters on a fluorescent background, those are signs alerting the cast and crew members where they need to go. Examples are QOTS, DANNY (which is NCIS New Orleans), and FONZO. The words or acronyms are typically referencing the production company or working title of the piece and are meant to be somewhat cryptic so that the general public is not aware of their presence.

additional ten cents to take a peek at the Edison Vitascope projector itself. Die-hard enthusiasts forked over another ten cents to leave with a scrap of film from the projector room floor.

The building has since been a bank and a Burger King, and now is VooDoo Mart convenience store. Efforts are in place to generate funds to install a historical marker in front of the building.

SEPARATE AND UNEQUAL

How did a local act of civil disobedience change the American landscape?

In 1892, Homer Plessy boarded a New Orleans train, sat down, and changed the world.

Plessy was sitting in the "whites only" section of the train, and as a person of color, he was legally obligated to sit in the "blacks only" section instead. Despite the fact that with his lighter complexion, Plessy was able to pass as white, the conductor somehow correctly divined his heritage and asked him to move. When he refused, a private investigator who happened to be sitting in the same car was immediately on hand to make the arrest.

If this all seems a bit contrived, it's because it was: Plessy, the conductor, the investigator, and even the train company were in contact with the Comité des Citoyens (Citizens' Committee), a nineteenth-century civil rights group that was trying to challenge the beginning of the Jim Crow era in Louisiana. They had arranged for both Plessy's act of disobedience and his arrest, needing an arrest on the books that they could challenge in court.

Unfortunately, the United States Supreme Court upheld the disputed law in 1896, and the case known as

---

When you're standing in front of this historical marker, turn around and look across the street. See the train tracks? These are the same tracks Homer's train would have traveled on in 1892.

Across the tracks you can also see several other murals and beautiful street art/graffiti. The yellow mural featuring the portrait of a black girl was done by local artist B-Mike—the building the mural is painted on is the artist's studio.

PRESS STREET RAILROAD YARD

What: A monument and park dedicated to civil rights hero Homer Plessy

Where: The corner of Royal St. and Press St. (now renamed Homer Plessy Way)

Cost: Free

Pro Tip: Those who would like to pay more personal respects to Homer Plessy can also do so at his grave—he is interred in Saint Louis Cemetery #1.

Plessy v. Ferguson would go down in infamy as the legal basis for segregation, creating what's now known as the "separate but equal" doctrine. This doctrine would eventually be overturned by *Brown v. Board of Education* in 1954, but sadly, Plessy would never see it happen—he passed away in 1925.

In 2009, however, the descendants of both Plessy and Ferguson (the Louisiana judge who had initially issued the verdict) formed the Plessy and Ferguson Foundation, a new civil rights organization. The foundation's first act? Setting a historic marker at the spot where Plessy had been arrested so many years ago, a long-overdue testament to one of America's first civil rights heroes.

A STORE HOUDINI COULD HAVE VISITED

What is the oldest business on Magazine Street?

Magazine Street has become a major shopping attraction in New Orleans. Many think that the stretch between Louisiana and Jackson Avenues is the best place to see some really fun and unique shops. One in particular is so old that it could have been visited by Houdini. Houdini went to locksmiths in the various cities he visited and even had a locksmith on his touring crew. In 1907, he performed his magic show and public displays of escapism for the crowds of New Orleans. By this time, a local locksmith had already been in business for sixty-two years.

H. Rault Locksmith, located at 3027 Magazine Street, has been in business since 1845 and is the second oldest locksmith in the United States, not to mention the oldest business on Magazine Street. Although we don't know if Houdini did business with H. Rault, the years of business match when Houdini was in New Orleans, so he very well could have paid a visit.

H. RAULT LOCKSMITH

What: A working locksmith that is also a museum and vintage gift shop

Where: 3027 Magazine St.

Cost: Free

Pro Tip: Michelle Miller, the owner, is often in the store. Her excitement for the history of H. Rault is infectious, and if she isn't busy, Michelle will regale visitors with stories about the history of the store.

H. Rault is considered one of Magazine Street's best-kept secrets. Visitors love snapping pictures of the keys

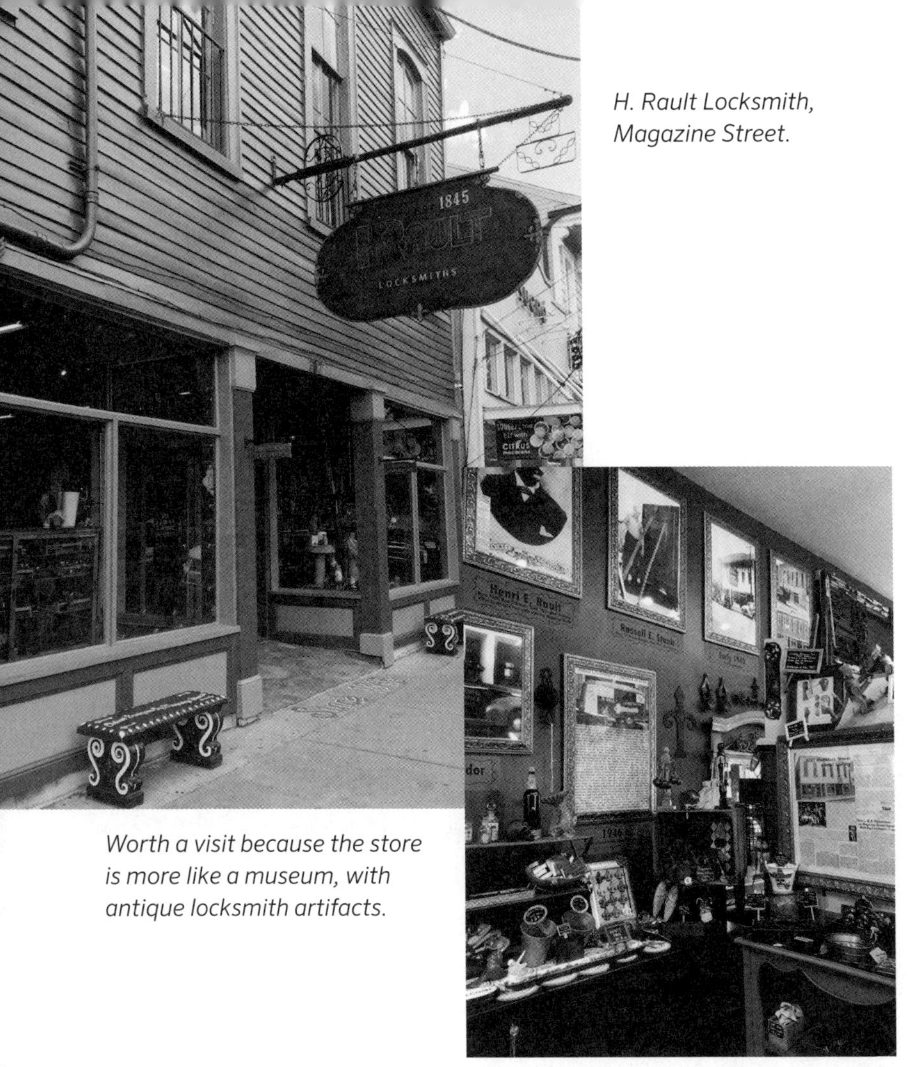

H. Rault Locksmith, Magazine Street.

Worth a visit because the store is more like a museum, with antique locksmith artifacts.

and locks in the concrete in front of the entrance as well as the "Rault 1845" spelled out with antique keys in the concrete a few feet from the entrance. There are very few experiences on Magazine Street quite like walking into H. Rault and taking a step back in time.

Although it seems like a museum, H. Rault is a full service locksmith. All of the old houses and locks in the city no doubt keep them quite busy.

HUCK-A-BUCK

How do locals cool off in the summer?

It's no secret that New Orleans gets quite hot in the summer. While the New Orleans Sno-ball is very well known, another way that locals cool off is to find someone selling Huck-a-buck. Huck-a-buck is simply a cup of frozen fruit juice or Kool-Aid. Also known as "frozen cup," Huck-a-buck is almost never found in stores or restaurants. Rather, it's made and sold by a random neighbor that the other neighbors know well. While tourists would have a hard time finding Huck-a-buck, there is one establishment that often has it in the summer. Across from Antoine's Restaurant on St. Louis Street, there is a little praline shop called Leah's Pralines, and while Huck-a-buck isn't advertised, they sell them for "a buck." This little secret is well known by the restaurant employees in the French Quarter. The flavors are typically cherry, lime, or pineapple and—like eating crawfish—everyone has their favorite method. Some break through with a spoon while others flip the ice bar over in the cup and lick it like a popsicle. There is no wrong way. In the summer it's not uncommon to see restaurant workers dressed in tuxedos eating Huck-a-buck while on break. It's especially common for Antoine's employees due to the proximity of Leah's to the restaurant.

Fitness guru Richard Simmons grew up on St. Louis Street and worked for Leah's when he was in high school.

A look inside Leah's Pralines.

HUCK-A-BUCK

What: A budget-friendly, frozen, summertime treat

Where: Leah's Pralines, 714 St. Louis St.

Cost: $1

Pro Tip: While in Leah's, ask for a sample of their famous bacon pecan brittle.

Sign outside of Leah's Pralines on St. Louis Street.

THE PERFECT STORM

How is a beloved weatherman connected to a classic cocktail?

Few things cause locals and tourists alike to make the face of disgust like suggesting a Hurricane cocktail. The red, uber-sweet, and ridiculously strong concoction has been the source of many a hangover in New Orleans over the years. But how can such a drink be so popular? The straight answer is that the hurricane served today isn't the same one that started the craze back in the 1940s.

Back in the '40s, the two owners of Pat O'Brien's bar, Charlie Cantrell and Benson "Pat" O'Brien, invented a wonderful cocktail with the overage of rum that they had in storage. Whiskey was hard to get at this time because of the war, but rum was plentiful and cheap. Simply by mixing rum, passion fruit syrup, and lemon juice, they created one of the most famous cocktails in New Orleans—the Hurricane. They served it in a glass shaped like a hurricane lantern and it quickly became the "cool" thing to be seen drinking.

The cocktail got so popular that it became harder to keep up with demand. To make things easier, the bar resorted to making large amounts of the cocktail mix so that all they had to do was quickly fill a glass with ice, pour, and serve. This is also when they introduced grenadine to the recipe, and the signature red drink became a thing.

Another great place for an original recipe Hurricane is Tiki Tolteca, located above Felipe's Mexican Taqueria on North Peters Street.

The Black Duck Bar, located in the Palace Cafe restaurant on Canal Street, is named after the most notorious Prohibition rum runner boat, which was used to nail other runners when it was finally captured by authorities.

THE NASH ROBERTS

What: The original Hurricane cocktail, a.k.a. the Nash Roberts

Where: The Black Duck Bar inside the Palace Cafe restaurant: 605 Canal St.

Cost: $11

Pro Tip: Rum aficionados should consider joining the New Orleans Rum Society through the Palace Cafe restaurant. More information, free rum tastings, and invitations to rum events in the city are offered to members.

The Black Duck Bar's version of the Hurricane—the Nash Roberts.

For those wishing to have an original Hurricane cocktail, a visit to the Black Duck Bar located on the second floor of the Palace Cafe restaurant should fit the bill. It's here where they make the original Hurricane, only they don't call it that. To prevent people from running away at the sound of the words "Hurricane cocktail," they decided to name the drink after one of New Orleans's most beloved meteorologists: Nash Roberts.

IGNATIUS REILLY STATUE

Where can you take a picture with the lead character of a Pulitzer Prize-winning novel?

In 1963, John Kennedy Toole wrote the novel *A Confederacy of Dunces*. Although it is required reading for many students today, it wasn't immediately respected. Toole was proud of his work and believed that others would enjoy it. He presented it to many reviewers, but few took the time to actually read it. He felt that he was going nowhere with the novel and in 1969 he took his own life. It was his mother who found the manuscript and continued presenting it for publication. Her final attempt was Loyola University in New Orleans where she insisted that Walker Percy read it. He reluctantly agreed and found the novel to be a work of genius. It was Percy who finally got the novel published in 1980. John Kennedy Toole would receive a posthumous Pulitzer Prize for fiction in 1981.

A Confederacy of Dunces is about the adventures of the slovenly main character, Ignatius Reilly. It's considered to be one of the best descriptions of New Orleans ever and is quite amusing for current New Orleans residents.

IGNATIUS REILLY STATUE

What: A life-size statue of the beloved NOLA character

Where: 819 Canal St.

Cost: Free

Pro Tip: After taking a picture of the statue, fans can walk over to Bourbon Street for a Lucky Dog!

Ignatius Reilly statue portrayed by John McConnell.

Fans of the story wishing to get a picture with Ignatius need only go to the 800 block of Canal Street on the French Quarter side. There, in the middle of the block, is the statue of Ignatius Reilly apparently walking out of what was once a department store. Fans of the book will immediately understand the statue's pose and the reason for the location.

Ignatius is depicted under the D.H. Holmes department store clock. Many locals have fond memories of this store.

INTERGALACTIC STAIRWAY

Where can you find a stairway to Wookieeville?

There are three blocks of lower Frenchmen Street that come alive at nighttime with New Orleans–style music, excellent food, and handmade art. Dat Dog restaurant fits right in. Diners can nosh on the best-tasting sausages while overseeing the street bands from the balcony. But to get up there, visitors partake in an unexpected adventure.

Standing at the base of the stairway, there is a lot to take in. Artwork adorns every inch of wall, ceiling, and stair space and is kept aglow by purple and pink lighting. Little green men on the right wall encourage the hesitant to approach the stairs with their large smiles and kind, glossy-black alien eyes. Midway up the stairs, the general outer space and planetary theme morphs into *Star Wars*, overseen by Jabba the Hutt's knowing grimace from the left. At the landing, look back to see cute kittens shooting laser beams from their death stare eye sockets. Turning forward again, follow the *Millennium Falcon* and go past the frightened Ewok (he is rightly so, with the *Aliens* mascot lurking above him), and into the dining room.

You, too, can join the Cult of the Sacred Drunken Wookiee! But why stop there? The Chewbacchus.org website has instructions on how to become an ordained ChewbacchanALIEN Minister, legally able to officiate weddings.

The Sacred Drunken Wookiee is a combination of Star War's Chewbacca and the Roman god of wine, Bacchus.

This is the den of the three-eyed, 3-D, Sacred Drunken Wookiee. In the corners are tiny Ewoks, watching from their forest houses of Endor. Above diners' heads are planets, solar systems, TIE fighters, X-Wings, and even the Starship *Enterprise*, since Dat Dog does not discriminate. Actually, there are nods to the whole genre of sci-fi. *Hitchhiker's Guide* fans will spot the giant number 42, and the Flying Spaghetti Monster even makes an appearance.

The design is a collaboration between Dat Dog and the sci-fi Mardi Gras Krewe known as The Krewe of Chewbacchus (a riff off the wine god Bacchus, who has a Krewe of his own). They parade during Mardi Gras in a rather mystical fashion, encouraging every member to show his/her inner nerd with pride.

DAT DOG UPSTAIRS

What: A sci-fi haven with excellent food and views

Where: 601 Frenchmen St.

Cost: $

Pro Tip: Any of the Chef's Specials are a sure win, but with twenty different "dogs" and twenty different toppings, diners can mix and match their favorites. Standout dogs are the alligator, duck, and fried chicken, and favorite toppings include the andouille sauce, crawfish étouffée, bacon, and homemade sauerkraut. Dat Dog is even a favorite with vegans.

RECORD, RINSE, REPEAT

Where can you do your laundry in the birthplace of rock 'n' roll?

Memphis might get to claim Sun Records and Elvis Presley, but Cosimo Matassa recorded everybody else in New Orleans. In 1945, Matassa, a Tulane University dropout, opened J&M Recording Studios on North Rampart Street with his business partner Joe Mancuso. Specializing in the uniquely New Orleanian rhythm and blues sound, the partners quickly attracted local musicians like Professor Longhair, Bobby Charles, and Fats Domino.

As these recordings played across the country, more and more independent labels arrived seeking the famous New Orleans sound. As these records were produced, a group of session musicians headed by Dave Bartholomew became the backbone of the J&M sound. Herb Hardesty would play tenor saxophone solos, setting the template for generations of rock 'n' roll songs. Earl Palmer, the group's drummer, is even credited

THE J&M RECORDING STUDIO

What: A laundromat sitting in the footprint of a Rock 'N' Roll Hall of Fame inductee landmark

Where: 840 North Rampart St.

Cost: Free to step inside and explore. Doing laundry? Bring a roll of quarters.

Pro Tip: Even if you have no laundry to wash, go inside for a moment. The laundromat still displays pictures, artifacts, and information from the recording studio's history and also has a retail space and art gallery in the front.

Although it's washers and dryers spinning now instead of records, the old J&M logo can still be seen on the floor of the front entrance. The building also boasts not one, but two historical plaques—one placed by the Historic Landmarks Commission and the other placed by the Rock and Roll Hall of Fame!

for inventing the backbeat—now the rhythmic foundation of the entire genre.

More musicians and more hits followed. Fats Domino's "The Fat Man," which some consider the first rock 'n' roll song, would be recorded at the studio in 1949. Little Richard's "Tutti Frutti" followed in 1955. Outside artists who went out of their way to record at J&M included Ray Charles, Big Joe Turner, and Jerry Lee Lewis. Local musicians Allen Toussaint, Dr. John, and Irma Thomas all visited early in their careers as well.

It wasn't just Cosimo Matassa's musical and engineering skill sets that drew everyone in—J&M studios was also a fully racially integrated studio during the height of the Jim Crow era. Though the studio closed in 1956, Matassa, Bartholomew, and Fats Domino would return in 1999 (on the golden anniversary of Domino's "The Fat Man") to commemorate the site—now a laundromat—as a historic landmark. Matassa himself was inducted into the Rock and Roll Hall of Fame in 2012.

Even though the J&M Studio was desegregated, it was the exception, not the rule. Many early musicians recall having to take their lunch breaks separately in segregated restaurants and diners, only to reunite back at the studio.

FIT FOR A KING (page 54)

AWASH IN HISTORY (page 148)

BOOZY CAKE (page 24)

ENTER THE ZONE (page 44)

BETTER THAN BEIGNETS? (page 14)

DRINK
ELIZABETH'S
REAL FOOD DONE REAL GOOD
601 Gallier 944-9272
FRESH SEAFOOD DAILY
BEER
PO BOYS
Eat

FIT FOR A COUNT (page 52)

BLACKENING MOTHERSHIP (page 18)

PRAYERS ANSWERED—SAME-DAY DELIVERY AVAILABLE (page 46)

SHAKEN, NOT STIRRED (page 160)

HISTORY UNBOUND (page 20)

MARDI GRAS INDIANS (page 116)

THE GHOST OF THE RED-LIGHT DISTRICT (page 106)

THE MOTHER OF ORPHANS (page 120)

SEPARATE AND UNEQUAL (page 74)

THE SHRINE OF THE VOODOO QUEEN (page 122)

AN ELDER AMONG THE ANCIENTS (page 180)

THE GHOST OF THE RED-LIGHT DISTRICT

How did one New Orleans madam manage to advertise from beyond the grave?

Even in death, the madam Josie Arlington mocked the families that looked down on her.

Having risen to both infamy and wealth as the "First Lady of Storyville" (Storyville was the legal red-light district of New Orleans until 1917), Josie's four-story brothel, The Arlington, was known far and wide as one of the most luxurious and expensive pleasure houses in the neighborhood. Despite her wealth, her profession meant she would never be truly accepted by the city's high-society dignitaries—even though many of them secretly visited her establishment.

Having been so ostracized, Josie decided she'd have the last laugh from beyond the grave. She used part of her wealth to build herself an extravagant red marble tomb in Metairie Cemetery, choosing her final resting place among the city's elite. The mausoleum's doors were framed by two columns capped by matching urns, each bearing carved renditions of the "eternal flame of life" (or the

---

Josie never told anyone who the bronze statue of the woman is supposed to be. Some think it represents a virgin being turned away at Josie's brothel. Others think it's Josie herself, being locked out of her family home by her father after he learned of her illicit occupation.

While the red-light phenomenon was quickly debunked, true believers swear they've seen the bronze statue animate and stroll through the cemetery after dark!

THE TOMB OF JOSIE ARLINGTON

What: The allegedly haunted grave of a famous New Orleans madam

Where: Metairie Cemetery, 5100 Pontchartrain Blvd. Josie's grave is in a lane to the left of the entrance, and the back of the tomb can be seen from the service road approaching the gates.

Cost: Free. Open 7 days/week, 8:30 a.m.- 5:00 p.m.

Pro Tip: The "Morales" name on the mausoleum indicates the current occupants; at some point along the way, Josie's tomb was sold and her remains moved to a nondisclosed location within the same graveyard.

torches of the red-light district, depending on the viewer's interpretation).

Josie died on Valentine's Day, 1914. Immediately following her burial, however, visitors began to notice something strange: at night, the two granite torches seemed to come alive and blaze with red light! Crowds began to gather to witness the phenomenon. Families with loved ones in neighboring tombs were mortified. The police were called. Josie seemed to be open for business, even from beyond the grave.

Unfortunately for would-be ghost hunters, this particular paranormal claim was debunked fairly easily: a cemetery worker eventually noticed that a nearby toll road's signal light was swaying in the breeze, and its reddish light was reflecting off the red marble, giving the tomb its supernatural appearance. Despite the light's removal, however, Josie's legend remained; her tomb is still cited as one of the city's most haunted locations.

JUMBO SHRIMP

How (and why) did shrimp boils start, and where can you attend one?

Talk about fresh seafood—today's technological advances allow people to eat shrimp that was swimming in the Gulf just a few hours prior! Shrimpers use infrared locator tools to precisely identify where the schools of shrimp are running before dropping their trolling nets. In a few hours, commercial shrimpers can harvest over one hundred pounds of shrimp, which are immediately refrigerated or flash frozen below deck. Once reaching shore, the shrimp are transported on ice or in climate-controlled trucks until they reach their final destination.

This is very different from how it used to be. A successful shrimping trip meant several days, not hours. It took much longer for shrimpers to locate the shrimp, relying simply on trial and error. Once harvested, the shrimp were placed on blocks of ice that would melt in about three days. This meant that shrimp caught early in

---

At Mister Gregory's Shrimp Boil, pay special attention to the texture and flavor of the shrimp. Because of their large size and superb flavor and toothsome texture, wild-caught Gulf shrimp are most often sold to Japan for sushi at $16 per pound and up. Most shrimp consumed in the United States are corn-fed, farmed shrimp with a spongy texture and very little flavor that are imported from China and Indonesia for $3 per pound.

Shrimp at Mister Gregory's Shrimp Boil.

the trip often emitted a less-than-pleasant odor.

To ensure the shrimp were safe to eat, they were boiled for a few *hours* with different spices and essential oils that were brought to New Orleans from the other European colonies in the Caribbean islands and North Atlantic trade route, especially cayenne pepper and clove oil (which was considered antiseptic). This produced shrimp that were rubbery in texture, fiery hot with cayenne, and tasting heavily of clove. The common perception was that this long, harsh cooking method killed any bacteria and made the shrimp safe to eat. It certainly succeeded in covering up the bad smell.

A shrimp boil today still consists largely of clove and cayenne flavoring. The older generations prefer the longer boil time out of (unnecessary) safety concerns, but the younger generations use a shorter cooking time for a more pleasing texture and the ability to taste the shrimp itself, along with the boil spices.

MR. GREGORY'S SHRIMP BOIL

What: Backyard-style shrimp boil with all the fixin's

Where: 806 N Rampart St.

Cost: $$$$

Pro Tip: Go hungry! The shrimp are large and plentiful, and you'll get all the appropriate side dishes plus an appetizer and dessert! It's BYOB, and be sure to be on time as the door opens and closes promptly at the posted starting time. The boil often includes live entertainment from a local singer, dancer, or drag queen.

RING AROUND THE JUDGE

What superstition is believed to keep French Quarter revelers out of jail?

New Orleans's French Quarter has long been a location of debauchery where people tend to throw inhibitions to the wind and let loose. Some people take this too far. Some go so far over the legal line that they find themselves nursing a hangover in jail the next morning. Mixing this trend with New Orleans mysticism and superstition, the people of New Orleans have invented some interesting rituals used for warding off arrest. One such ritual is reputed to keep revelers out of jail for the evening. The first step is to find the statue of Justice Edward White, located just outside of the Louisiana Supreme Court building on the Royal Street side.

White was a United States senator, and in 1910 he was appointed Chief Justice of the Supreme Court. He is famous for his involvement in the *Plessy v. Ferguson* case as well as for his landmark decision upholding the constitutionality of the draft.

It is a well-known superstition that finding the statue and running around it counter clockwise three times

---

Justice White was a Confederate Civil War soldier. It is said that he was captured, but some historians question this, as his name was never listed among the list of captured Confederate soldiers.

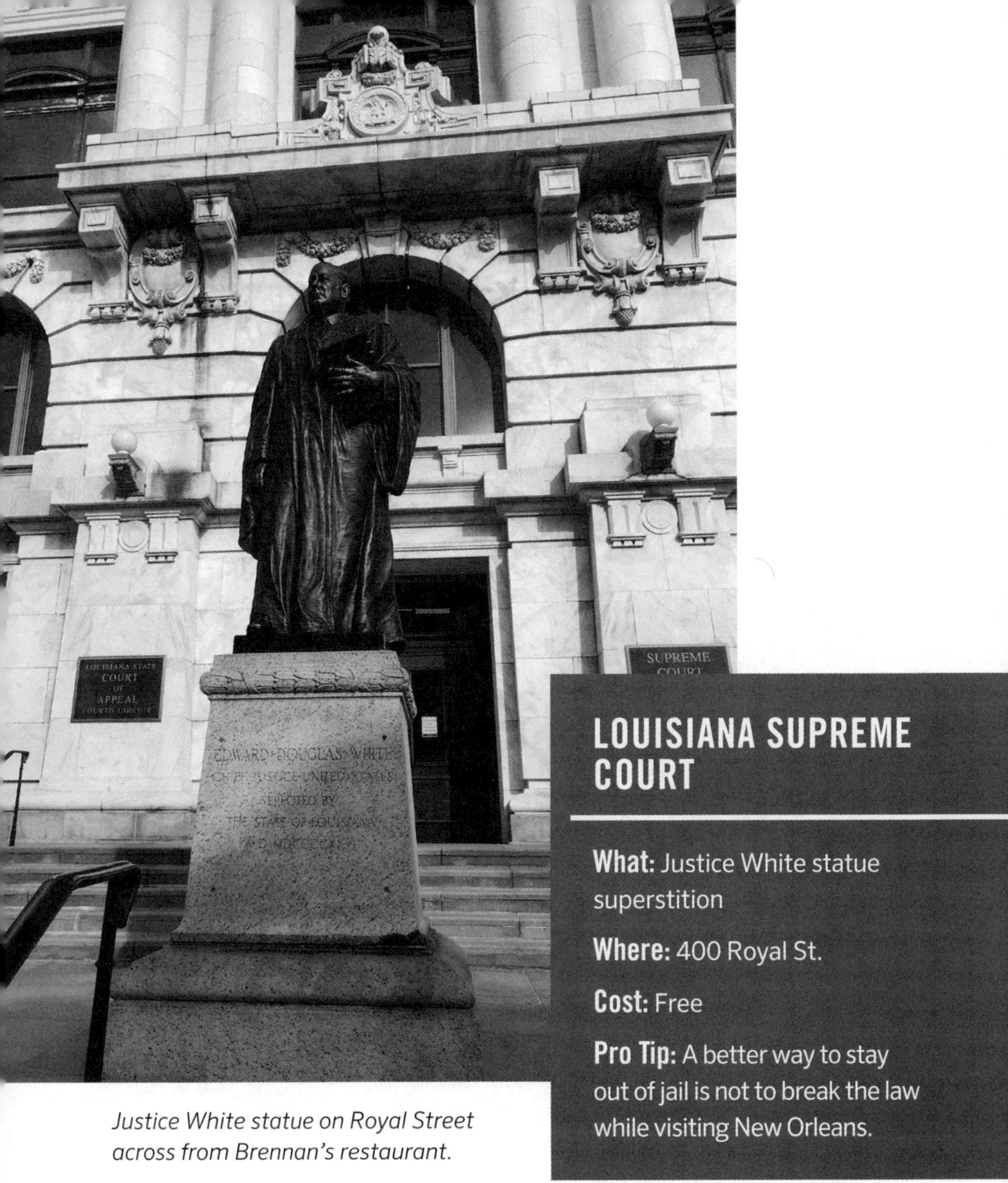

Justice White statue on Royal Street across from Brennan's restaurant.

LOUISIANA SUPREME COURT

What: Justice White statue superstition

Where: 400 Royal St.

Cost: Free

Pro Tip: A better way to stay out of jail is not to break the law while visiting New Orleans.

protects one from being arrested that evening. While few accept the validity of this antic, people continue to do it while thinking, "better safe than sorry."

No one knows who started the superstition or when, but it is alive and well to this day.

X MARKS THE STORM

Why are there Xs spray-painted on residential houses, and what do they mean?

Though more than a decade has passed since Hurricane Katrina, some evidence of the storm still remains. One of the most common remnants is also one that outsiders find confusing: large, spray-painted Xs on the sides of buildings with numbers and shorthand abbreviations surrounding it. For many, the "Katrina X" is the clearest visual reminder of the storm and its aftermath, and each one bears a hidden story.

When first responders performed search-and-rescue operations immediately following the hurricane, they needed a way to communicate with one another. With the power still out and so many independent organizations arriving to help, large-scale coordination was impossible. Instead, the responders used the graffiti as a way to communicate the who, when, and what to all other groups that followed after.

THE "KATRINA X"

What: The graffiti that communicated information during search-and-rescue after Katrina

Where: Though the Xs can be found anywhere, two are close to other points of interest in this book: One sits at 1122 Jackson Ave., not far from the Buckner Mansion, and another can be seen on the Flooded House Museum itself.

Cost: Free

Pro Tip: These days, the Xs are as much a symbol of the city as the fleur-de-lis, and they can be found on everything from T-shirts to bumper stickers. The N-O-L-A that often replaces the typical shorthand stands for (of course) New Orleans, LA.

This shotgun house not only retained its X, it also still shows lingering damage from Katrina, 15 years after the storm.

The X was a quick way to divide the blank canvas of an outside wall into four quadrants. Starting at the west quadrant, the unit would abbreviate their own affiliations: NOPD for local police, LSP for state troopers, etc. Moving clockwise around the X, the north quadrant would indicate the date the house was searched, and the east quadrant indicated potential hazards inside the building (GL for gas leak; RATS for, well, rats). The southern quadrant indicated the number of people—living and dead—discovered inside.

Post-Katrina, some locals painted over the Xs immediately, preferring not to be reminded of the devastation of the storm. Others restored everything in the home except the graffiti, leaving it as a testament to the city's resilience. Some even got the X tattooed on their bodies, a permanent reminder of everything they endured. Whatever its personal meaning, the graffiti remains uniquely New Orleanian. FEMA has since made official changes to its search-and-rescue policies, and now uses similarly coded stickers and decals instead.

When you see a date included, do the math and count how many days there are between that date and August 29. That's how long the house stood in floodwaters before any first responders arrived.

LIGHTING THE WAY

Why is there a lighthouse in the middle of downtown New Orleans?

No, the light doesn't reach all the way to the Mississippi River (and even if it did, there's the not-so-small matter of a few skyscrapers in the way). No, the river didn't change course; there's never been a lake or other body of water next door; and no, it wasn't built during one of New Orleans's many flood seasons (though locals might offer up this explanation as a tongue-in-cheek criticism of the city's Sewerage & Water Board). Instead, the lighthouse that stands on Camp Street was designed to metaphorically light the way for a particular group of New Orleanians: the blind.

The Louisiana Commission for the Blind purchased the building on Camp Street in 1924 and soon afterward added the lighthouse as a symbol of their goal: providing employment and "lighting the way" for the visually handicapped of New Orleans. Once the new building was finished, it was renamed the Lighthouse for the Blind and provided services, education, and (most importantly) employment for the visually impaired.

The lighthouse was originally designed to resemble yet another lighthouse in New Orleans that now serves no navigational function: the Milneburg/ Port Ponchartrain lighthouse, which sits on the University of New Orleans campus.

While Lighthouse Louisiana has become exactly what its founders intended—a beacon of hope for the visually impaired—the lighthouse itself now stands empty. It's sometimes used as an event venue or for a pop-up business.

THE CBD LIGHTHOUSE

What: The Lighthouse for the Blind in downtown New Orleans

Where: 743 Camp St.

Cost: Free

Pro Tip: Though the Camp Street building is usually inaccessible, lighthouse enthusiasts can tour the New Canal Lighthouse at 8001 Lakeshore Drive, which features a replica of an 1839 lighthouse as well as a museum and education center.

By the 1950s, the lighthouse was put up for sale as the organization moved to larger facilities, and several businesses have come and gone (the building was vacant at the time of this writing). While many locals have forgotten its original purpose, the lighthouse's symbolism still drives the old organization's mission. Now renamed "Lighthouse Louisiana," the commission operates out of New Orleans, Baton Rouge, and Gulfport, Mississippi, and still provides Braille textbooks, operates a mobile eye clinic, and offers classes and training for the blind, not just in New Orleans but throughout the Gulf Coast region.

MARDI GRAS INDIANS

Why do African Americans dress up like Native Americans?

There is a very rich part of the African American culture in New Orleans that most visitors do not see. Just three days each year, African-descended men and women don elaborate and colorful Native American-like costumes and headdresses that they painstakingly design and hand sew. Feathers, plumes, beads, and stones adorn each suit from head to toe. Their creation requires an entire year's worth of time, money, and labor to construct, only to be worn three times before it is retired forever.

Why do they do it? It is in homage to the Native Americans who sheltered and nurtured escaped slaves. It is a celebration of beauty and life amidst the African American struggle. It is a legacy, and it has been a tradition since the 1800s.

When the various "tribes" take to the streets, New Orleanians search the neighborhoods to find them. They will follow a tribe until two tribes meet, which is when the show begins. It is a standoff of chants, dancing, and singing in an African–Native American fusion style, culminating when each tribe's Big Chief struts his "suit" to determine which is the "prettiest." Once the encounter is over, the

---

For a better idea of the music, look up "The Golden Eagles Indian Red Live." This is the song—a prayer of sorts—that every tribe sings as they take to the streets.

Left: Thousands of tiny seed beads depict animals, symbols, or even entire landscape scenes on each forty-pound costume. Right: Close-up of hand-sewn beadwork.

tribes continue on their way until another tribe is spotted and the "fight" begins anew.

To see the Mardi Gras Indians (also called Masked Indians) perform outside of the three street performance days (Mardi Gras Day, St. Joseph's Day, and Super Sunday), check music schedules for band names with "Big Chief" or "Indian" in it. Their street music, such as hit song "Iko-Iko," significantly influenced what has become known as New Orleans rhythm and blues. One can also visit the Backstreet Cultural Museum or The House of Dance & Feathers to learn more about this culture and see the amazing suits up close.

BACKSTREET CULTURAL MUSEUM

What: An elaborate collection of handmade costumes celebrating a unique tradition

Where: 1116 Henriette DeLille St.

Cost: $

Pro Tip: The House of Dance & Feathers in the Lower Ninth Ward (appointment required) is another excellent place to visit.

IT'S A MARDI GRAS WORLD, AFTER ALL

Where can you see Carnival being made year-round?

Roy Kern and his son Blaine built their very first Mardi Gras float in 1932, cobbling together what materials and paints they could afford to decorate the back of a mule-drawn garbage wagon. Roy was an artist trying to support his family during the Great Depression by painting signs and lettering the bows of freighters and barges traveling the Mississippi River.

In 1947, struggling to pay his mother's medical bills, Blaine followed in his father's footsteps and offered to paint a mural in the hospital in exchange for medical services. A surgeon in the hospital, impressed with the mural, invited Blaine to design and build floats for a local Mardi Gras Krewe (social club). With that, Kern Studios was born, and Blaine set out on a life path that would eventually see him known locally as "Mister Mardi Gras."

Apprenticing with float builders and costume makers throughout Europe, Blaine returned to New Orleans to revolutionize the parades with double-decker floats,

MARDI GRAS WORLD

What: A tourable workshop where Carnival floats are constructed/displayed year-round

Where: 1380 Port of New Orleans Place

Cost: Tours run 9:30–4:30, 7 days/week. Adult tickets are $22 with discounts available.

Pro Tip: Have a lot of friends? Mardi Gras World offers private, after-hours tours for groups of ten or more.

The floats on display are mostly provided by the Krewe of Rex. The Rex parade rolls on Mardi Gras Day itself, and since rex means "king" in Latin, the King of Rex each year is considered to be the "king of kings"—in other words, the most important figure in Mardi Gras Royalty and the King of Carnival itself (most of us have to resign ourselves to playing Jester).

animatronics, and flashy lights (Disney once tried to recruit him to develop these same concepts in their theme parks!). At the same time, he leveraged Kern Studios into a financial powerhouse. While a float made in the studio's early years might cost $5,000, in 2013 the studio debuted a 370-foot-long float worth $1.5 million!

After countless requests for tours of the studios and more than a few eager locals got caught trying to get a sneak peek of an under-construction Carnival, Kern Studios opened Mardi Gras World to provide the public with a behind-the-scenes look at the making of New Orleans's biggest spectacles. Blaine has since retired, but his legacy lives on; the studio is now operated by his son, Barry, and grandson, Fitz.

After more than sixty years, the Krewe of Rex shocked the city when they announced that they would no longer be using Kern Studios for their floats' construction. Kern Studios will continue to build and design floats for other "super krewes," including Endymion, Bacchus, Orpheus, Zulu, and Muses.

THE MOTHER OF ORPHANS

...and packaged crackers?

Born in 1813 in Tully, Ireland, Margaret (nee Gaffney) moved to Baltimore at the age of five. Just four years later, she was orphaned. Reared by a kind Welsh family, she married Charles Haughery and moved to New Orleans at age twenty-one in 1835. Poor Margaret's hardships followed her south; her husband and infant daughter died just one year later. Again on her own, she turned her focus outward.

Young Margaret was a laundress at the posh St. Charles Hotel. When not working, she solicited businesses for food, clothes, and money for orphaned children. The Sisters of Charity provided her a room at the Poydras Orphan Asylum in exchange for her efforts. But she wanted to do more. Distraught that there was no milk for the children, Margaret saved her meager wages and bought a dairy cow. Her farm livestock numbers increased to forty cows over the next two years, according to business receipts in the archdiocesan archives.

In 1859, Margaret bought a bakery that was located on present-day South Peters Street. Her main purpose was to

---

Despite her eventual wealth, Our Margaret never lived in a mansion or owned lavish tangibles. She instead stayed in a small apartment attached to her bakery, and anyone who needed help could approach her as she sat in her rocking chair on the front porch.

Margaret's Steam and Mechanical Bakery was one of the first steam bakeries in the country. This ad ran in a local newspaper, L'Abeille, *on July 17, 1869.*

provide bread to the orphans, and eventually her product line expanded to cakes, cookies, macaroni, and more. "The Bread Woman of New Orleans" took her business to the next level when she invented a way to package crackers and ship them "fresh" to clients in other cities.

Margaret Haughery died on February 9, 1882, having provided funds for three new orphan asylums during her lifetime and leaving another $50,000 (a sizeable fortune) to charity. Her funeral attendees ranged from the mayor, archbishop, and state governors to thousands of orphans who mourned "our Margaret." A statue of Haughery was erected in her honor, and she is currently being considered for sainthood by the Catholic Church, due to her relentless caretaking of orphaned children, regardless of their color, political alliance, or religion—all things that were quite controversial at that time.

MARGARET HAUGHERY STATUE

What: A statue of Margaret with orphans, which was the second statue in the United States erected for a woman

Where: 1142 Margaret Place

Cost: Free

Pro Tip: Thirsty? Nearby are lots of excellent options! Grab a coffee at local favorite French Truck Coffee (their original location!). Or cool off with a microbrew from Courtyard Brewery or a cocktail from Barrel Proof. All are just two blocks away from the statue (on Margaret's right side is Camp Street; follow that one block behind her to Erato Street and turn left).

THE SHRINE OF THE VOODOO QUEEN

Where do the locals pay respect to the city's most infamous resident?

Not even death could diminish Marie Laveau's celebrity. As the undisputed "Voodoo Queen" of New Orleans in the nineteenth century, Marie had built a reputation as a healer, an advocate of social justice, and a devout Catholic. Depending on whom you asked, she was also known as an information broker, wielder of dark arts, and mysterious cult leader. Nevertheless, when she was interred in Saint Louis Cemetery #1 in 1881, her tomb quickly became an attraction of its own, with both tourists and religious practitioners alike leaving offerings, taking pictures, and paying their respects.

In 2015, after increasingly frequent incidents of vandalism, the Archdiocese of New Orleans had to restrict access to Saint Louis Cemetery #1, requiring all visitors who were not related to the interred to enter only with a licensed tour guide. Again, Marie Laveau was at the center of the controversy: this change was precipitated by

---

Glassman's voodoo community also holds several religious ceremonies and rituals that are open to the general public. Notable dates include the head-washings on June 23 (a ritual that, in part, pays respect to Marie Laveau) and the Fete Gede (or Festival of the Ancestors) on November 1.

Because no photographs of Marie Laveau exist, every rendition is simply the artist's best guess. Though most accounts describe her as being very fair-skinned by virtue of her mixed-race heritage, a few depictions (including this one) chose to depict her with a darker complexion, a nod to her importance within the black communities of New Orleans.

a particularly brazen vandal who had painted Marie's entire tomb with a layer of bright pink paint. The removal of the latex paint nearly destroyed the tomb, and the restrictions were put in place soon afterward.

With a paywall suddenly blocking the Voodoo community's access to one of their most beloved icons, local priestess Sallie Ann Glassman reached out to artist Ricardo Pustanio, who created a papier-mâché statue of Marie as the centerpiece of a living, evolving art installation dedicated to both the priestess and her misunderstood religion. A replica of her tomb was soon added, and prayer candles and offerings began appearing immediately—some added by Glassman and her community, others spontaneously added by other locals, tourists, and Voodooists.

THE INTERNATIONAL SHRINE OF MARIE LAVEAU

What: A spiritual and artistic installation dedicated to Marie Laveau, the Voodoo Queen

Where: The New Orleans Healing Center, 2372 St. Claude Ave.

Cost: Free

Pro Tip: Didn't bring an offering? The Island of Salvation Botanica (also in the Healing Center) is a local voodoo shop and sells candles, herbs, and other voodoo-related items.

BOOKSHELVES TO HISTORY

Where can one find a hidden cache of antiques?

Royal Street has long been a destination for those wishing to enjoy antique shopping. Businesses with some of the oldest and rarest antiques can be found on just about every block. There is one particular store with the distinction of being voted best antique store in New Orleans, and it has a secret.

M.S. Rau Antiques, located at 630 Royal Street, was opened in 1912 as a small antiques shop among the many on Royal. It has since grown to 25,000 square feet, and there are plans for further expansion. Treasures such as Norman Rockwell and Renoir paintings and rare objects such as an original Robert-Houdin mystery clock and a camel saddle made for Napoleon's army can all be found here. But there is one part of this massive store where the super valuable items are kept.

Toward the rear of the store there is one room that looks like an unassuming library. A closer look at what seems like a wall of books reveals that it isn't a wall of books at all. Instead it is actually a picture of a wall of books. Toward the center is a door handle, and behind this camouflaged door lay countless artifacts on multiple floors.

Since M.S. Rau's inventory is constantly changing, one never knows what treasures can be found when visiting.

M.S. Rau Antiques, located on Royal Street.

M.S. RAU ANTIQUES

What: A secret back room filled with world-reknowned paintings and artifacts that are all for sale

Where: 630 Royal St.

Cost: Free

Pro Tip: If the reader is truly in the market for antiques, deciding quickly on an item that one is interested in is important. Since Rau's clientele comes from around the world, items come and go in a flash.

For the most complete experience, ask one of the employees for a tour as he/she will be able to point out items that might evade the first-timer's eye.

MS WHY?

Why are the call letters for the New Orleans International Airport MSY?

Most people flying into New Orleans pay little attention to the three-letter code used to name the New Orleans International Airport: MSY. While most know that the name of the airport is the Louis Armstrong International Airport, the three-letter identifier MSY seems to make no sense. The fact is that it wasn't called the Louis Armstrong International Airport until it was renamed in August 2001. Prior to that, the airport was named the Moisant International Airport after John Moisant, an aviator famous for building the first all metal aircraft, participating in barnstorming races, and being the first to fly paying customers across the English Channel. Although that explains the M, what about the SY?

In 1910, John Moisant was in New Orleans seeking to top an aviation record of longest time and distance in the air. The previous record was 362 miles over 7 hours and 48 minutes, and Moisant was determined to better this time since the record was achieved only one day prior. He was in City Park for an air show, and after the show he was to fly to an airstrip in Kenner, Louisiana, only

LOUIS ARMSTRONG AIRPORT

What: MSY call letters for the international airport in New Orleans

Where: 900 Airline Dr., Kenner, Louisiana

Cost: Free

Pro Tip: Locals are allowed into the terminal with a guest pass that must be requested 24 hours in advance.

Louis Armstrong International Airport or MSY.

The new MSY opened in October 2019.

twelve miles away. From there the plan was for him to take off again and officially start his journey to beat the record. As he was about to land in Kenner, a gust of wind blew his plane over, dropping him to the ground. He was rushed to the hospital, where he was pronounced dead. Because of all of his accomplishments in his somewhat short career, it was agreed in 1946 to build an airport on the land where the accident happened and name it after John Moisant. So where does the SY come from? At the time of the accident that land was used as stock yards. MSY stands for Moisant Stock Yards.

The new MSY airport has a focus on top-notch New Orleans restaurants. If a traveler does not have time to dine in the city, he or she has plenty of New Orleans favorites to choose from inside the terminal.

TUGGING AT HEART (AND PUPPET) STRINGS

How did personal tragedy lead to one of the city's most unique performance venues?

Pandora Gastelum found her inspiration in the most unlikely of places.

Born in Texas, she had already studied and performed musical theater, stagecraft, and puppeteering in New York City, Prague, Florence, Bangkok, and Taipei, but like so many creative visionaries, found her real home in New Orleans. Unfortunately, a move to the city in 2004 was immediately beset by both public and personal tragedies: Hurricane Katrina displaced the puppeteer in 2005, and in 2007 she found herself orphaned.

Returning to a devastated city, she decided to convert her grief into an ambitious project: using her inheritance, she renovated a building in the New Marigny neighborhood into a small performance space, christening the new venue The Mudlark Public Theater. "A Mudlark," to hear Pandora describe it, "is a Dickensian term for orphan, specifically those that hunt for treasure in the gutter." It seemed the perfect metaphor for both her personal situation and the

---

You can see one of Pandora's favorite puppets inside the theater. "Whenever I get frustrated in a build," said the puppeteer, "I look to this giant swan and remember I made its neck from a pool noodle. There is always a solution, and it's usually simple!"

Pandora Gastelum (left) performs with several of her own creations alongside other members of the Mudlark Puppeteers. Many of these puppets (and others) are put on display in the theater after their production is finished.

overall Sysyphian atmosphere of artists and performers struggling post-Katrina.

The theme resonated throughout the creative community, and other "mudlarks" soon arrived. Today, the theater hosts an ever-rotating cast of musicians, artists, bohemians, and (of course) puppeteers, with Pandora's own Mudlark Puppeteers operating as the theater's resident company. As a company, the Mudlark Puppeteers present "original stories of heroic misfits and wayward love," and the same themes that created the theater often drive its puppets' narratives: sudden displacement, questions of identity, and reinvention.

"We imagine hope in the form of new stories, [with] the dispossessed as emerging heroes." The theme certainly seems to resonate: the Mudlark Theater celebrated its seventh annual New Orleans Giant Puppet Fest in 2019, now a national favorite for both performers and attendees worldwide.

THE MUDLARK PUPPET THEATER

What: A local puppeteer's bohemian performance venue

Where: 1200 Port St. Check online for show schedules (most shows start around 8 p.m.).

Cost: Varies by show, but tickets typically run from $5 to $20 per person

Pro Tip: Like many theaters, the Mudlark has a resident ghost. This particular spirit appreciates offerings of hard candy—you can see the theater's handmade altar (and leave an offering of your own!) opposite the bar.

MURDER AND MERCHANDISING

Where was the country's first celebrity auction?

Beautiful Jackson Square exists today thanks to a father-daughter duo. Businessman Andreas Almonester y Rojas paid for the rebuilding of the St. Louis Cathedral, Cabildo, and most of the Presbytère after the Great Fire of 1788 destroyed them. His sole descendent, daughter Micaela, inherited her father's immense wealth upon his death. She married into the Pontalba family and moved to France, where she was coerced into signing her family fortune over to her husband. Micaela's father-in-law, the Baron de Pontalba, tried to murder her to keep her from ever reclaiming her fortune. Believing she would surely die from her injuries, he committed suicide before the police arrived.

Despite taking three bullets in her chest and falling down a staircase, Micaela survived the brutal attack. The courts ruled in her favor, and she did reclaim that inheritance money along with her father's land in New Orleans.

The Pontalba Apartment buildings are some of the oldest apartment buildings in the country. They were the first to showcase intricate cast iron fence work, making Micaela responsible for starting the trend in New Orleans as a method for homeowners to display their wealth.

The Upper Pontalba Apartment building, one of the oldest apartment buildings in the country. Lind stayed in the corner unit, closest to the Cabildo.

Newly a Baroness, Micaela Almonester Pontalba moved back to New Orleans in 1849 and built the Upper and Lower Pontalba apartment buildings, which flank the right and left side of Jackson Square. She also converted the dirt lot between them into the magnificent park it is today.

In 1851, Micaela hosted the most famous celebrity in the world at her Parisian-style apartment building: Swedish opera star Jenny "The Nightingale" Lind. Seeing the popularity of Jenny Lind merchandise like gloves, paper dolls, furniture, and even Jenny Lind sausages, Micaela stripped Jenny's room of everything when she left—even the chamber pot—and sold them at auction from the very balcony on which Jenny had shyly waved hello to her adoring fans. Micaela had inherited her father's money and his business savvy, and since Jenny Lind was the first true celebrity in the United States, Micaela held what would be the first celebrity auction in the country.

UPPER PONTALBA APARTMENT BUILDING

What: First celebrity auction from a balcony

Where: 1008 N. Peters St.

Cost: Free

Pro Tip: Across Chartres Street from the building is Tableau Restaurant. Not only is it a great place to dine or grab a drink, it also has a hand-carved replica of the Pontalba Apartment staircases.

DINING THAT WILL LIFT YOUR SPIRITS

Why is there a table set for dinner in the stairwell at Muriel's restaurant?

New Orleans is an old city with a wild and yet very interesting past. Its historic architecture is appreciated and well protected, and this allows one to get a feel for life during recent centuries in the Big Easy. It's no secret that over the years there have been many stories of ghosts haunting the buildings. One of the most haunted restaurants in the French Quarter is Muriel's, located just steps from the St. Louis Cathedral. Muriel's offers classic Creole dishes and is quite popular, but the food isn't the only reason for its popularity: it's the secrets harbored within.

THE GHOST TABLE

What: Mr. Lepardi's table at Muriel's restaurant

Where: 801 Chartres St.

Cost: $$$ Depends on what you order for dinner

Pro Tip: Be sure to go up the stairs and pay a visit to the seance room for a drink in a very strange space.

In 1814, the building was the home of Mr. Pierre Antoine Lepardi. He was a wealthy man who loved his home but also loved gambling. During a poker game one evening, he bet his house and sadly lost. He was so distraught that he went upstairs and hanged himself.

Over the years, the building was bought and sold until it was finally turned into a restaurant. It is said that servers experienced items going missing, and some things were even observed flying across various dining rooms. This was

Muriel's restaurant located on Jackson Square.

clearly an unhappy spirit that wanted people out. Could it be Lepardi's spirit?

An investigation into the history of the building and the life of Lepardi revealed how much Lepardi enjoyed entertaining. One night the staff decided to set a table for Mr. Lepardi, and amazingly, all paranormal activity ceased. All they needed to do was acknowledge his presence and prepare a place for him. Since then, a table has been set each night for the spirit of Mr. Lepardi, and there have been no more reports of violent activity. That table can be seen in the stairwell leading to the seance room upstairs. One secret is that for the right price you can request to be seated at Mr. Lepardi's table for dinner. The experience can be a bit unnerving for some, which is why it isn't openly advertised.

Those wishing to see the ghost table but do not plan to eat in the restaurant need only peer through the gates of the carriageway and focus on the back stairwell. Many ghost tours stop here for the same vantage point.

IT TAKES A VILLAGE TO PERFORM

Where can you find (and play!) New Orleans's largest musical installation?

New Orleans already had the reputation of being a city built on music, but Jay Pennington and Delaney Martin took the idea a little more literally than most.

In 2011, the pair had already founded New Orleans Airlift, an organization designed to help musicians devastated by Hurricane Katrina. One of Airlift's earliest projects was the conversion of a collapsed eighteenth-century house into a combination performance venue and artistic installation. Originally conceived of as a single project, the idea quickly blossomed into the Music Box Village, an entire collection of shacks, tree houses, and structures that not only provide a place for musicians to perform, but in all cases double as unique instruments themselves!

The Japanese-style pagoda plays a secretly amplified steel guitar slide when its doors are opened or closed, and the floorboards double as piano keys. The "Bower's Nest"

Four times a year, the musical village becomes an art market instead, with over forty local artists exhibiting their work. Though the dates vary, the occasions do not. You can visit the Halloween market, the Christmas/Holiday market, the Easter market, and (of course) the Mardi Gras market!

New Orleans musicians play both their instruments and their stages during Blato Zlato's Voyager show in 2017. Utilizing an enormous cross-section of musicians (including the 9th Ward Marching Band, pictured) and a local dance troupe, the live show imagined the discovery of the Voyager album by an alien civilization. (Photo credit: Sarah Danziger)

houses enormous wind chimes (each helpfully labeled with the musical note it produces) that can be played via mallet or, sometimes, by Mother Nature herself. The old phone booth that sits in the middle of the Village has no outside line—instead it sends the speaker's voice to a rotating selection of speakers scattered throughout the venue.

When the Village opened in 2016, its aesthetic and uniqueness captured the imagination of musicians far and wide. Local rapper Big Freedia has performed there, as have Norah Jones, Gogol Bordello, and even the Louisiana Philharmonic Orchestra. Often the performances are as unique as the venue itself: local band Blato Zlato, for instance, once used the Village (and the help of forty other musicians) to recreate the Voyager "Golden Record," the music that accompanies NASA's Voyager interstellar probes.

THE MUSIC BOX VILLAGE

What: An interactive performance venue and installation

Where: 4557 N. Rampart St.

Cost: Varies by performance, but some public hours are also available for a suggested donation of $12/adult and $5/child

Pro Tip: Headed to a performance? Bring chairs and blankets, not coolers. The Village has a full bar on-site, and the unique layout of the space sometimes limits the space for seating.

AND THE BAND PLAYS ON...

How is one family of musicians helping their contemporaries even beyond death?

Lloyd Washington had a problem, and it wasn't even that he was dead. It was that after death, he had nowhere to go!

The well-known vocalist of the Ink Spots had passed on June 22, 2004, and had done so with no final resting place and few funds for his loved ones to use to build one. Instead, his cremated remains were held for three months in a makeshift shrine at one of his favorite bars (fellow jazz contemporary Ernie K-Doe's Mother-in-Law Lounge).

While many musicians would be happy to remain in their favorite venues forever, Lloyd's passing was the catalyst for an idea that had been brewing for six years: the creation of the New Orleans Musicians Tomb. The Barbarin family, one of the oldest and most prominent jazz families in New Orleans, agreed to donate six vaults in their family's large tomb structure so that local musicians would have a final resting place if no other options were available.

When Lloyd's funeral service was finally held in October 2004, he joined several luminaries who were already interred in the family vault: Isidore Barbarin, leader of the

---

The yellow building on the other side of St. Louis Street (once part of the Basin Street train station) is now a tourist information center where you can cool off, get a bottle of water, and use the public facilities.

The most notable feature of the tomb can be seen without entering the graveyard. Walk along St. Louis Street to the back of the cemetery, and the wrought iron cross bearing a stained-glass "blue note" of jazz can be seen rising above the interred.

Onward Brass Band (and a man whom Louis Armstrong called "Pops"), and Rose Barbarin Barker Colombel, mother of famous musician and teacher Danny Barker. Since 2004, other greats have joined them, including actor-drummer Bernard "Bunchy" Johnson; Fats Domino's manager, Billy Diamond; and Dr. Jack McConnell, co-founder of the New Orleans Musicians Clinic.

But it was Lloyd who got it started. The legal documents necessary to transfer the tombs were even signed in his presence (in a matter of speaking), at the Mother-in-Law Lounge. "So that means Lloyd can go in the tomb?" Antoinette K-Doe asked after the papers were signed. "Good," she continued. "I'm tired of him sleeping in here."

THE NEW ORLEANS MUSICIANS TOMB

What: A tomb specifically set aside for New Orleans musicians

Where: Back right quadrant of Saint Louis Cemetery #1, 425 Basin St.

Cost: Requires a guided tour to visit; tours begin at the cemetery gate for $20/person

Pro Tip: The cemetery can get quite hot, especially in the brutal summer humidity. We recommend bottled water (other beverages are not allowed inside the cemetery) and sunscreen!

THE FACE OF NEW ORLEANS'S FRENCH PAST

What did Napoleon look like?

The Cabildo is a building located on Jackson Square in the French Quarter. It was built just before the nineteenth century and served as the seat of all government in New Orleans. Today it is a museum that focuses on New Orleans history. One artifact in particular shows the face of a man imbedded not only in New Orleans history but also in world history. While most historic figures are depicted in paintings, this artifact is much more accurate because it's much more than just a painting: It is a death mask. But it's not just any death mask—it is the face of Napoleon. Death masks were used before the invention of photography to preserve the likeness of important people as accurately as possible. Once the person in question died, plaster was applied to the face making a mold, which was then filled to make the solid replica of the person's face. Often multiple masks were made and sent to far-off places to ensure that the true face was never forgotten. Looking

NAPOLEON'S FACE

What: Napoleon's death mask

Where: The Cabildo, 701 Chartres St.

Cost: $6

Pro Tip: If the Cabildo whets your appetite for New Orleans history, head to the other side of the Cathedral for a visit to the Presbytère. Here one can learn about Mardi Gras and Katrina.

The Cabildo in Jackson Square.

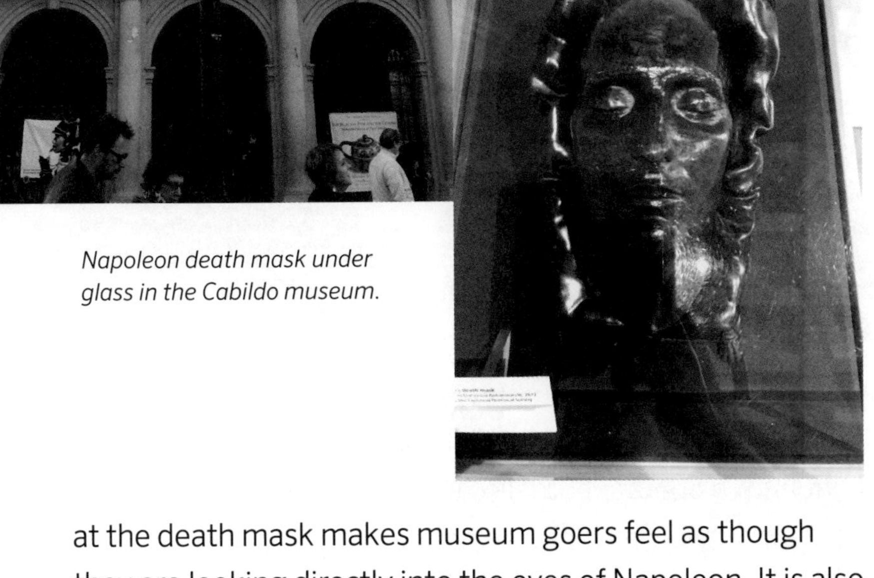

Napoleon death mask under glass in the Cabildo museum.

at the death mask makes museum goers feel as though they are looking directly into the eyes of Napoleon. It is also a reminder of New Orleans's French heritage. Napoleon was beloved in New Orleans, as it was a French colony until it was given to Spain in the early 1760s...and even then, the people, culture, and language remained primarily French!

When standing in the Cabildo, it is important to realize that the building was the site of the Louisiana Purchase transfer and the *Plessy v. Ferguson* civil rights court case.

THE TRICKS OF THE TRADE

Where can you see the last traces of New Orleans's infamous red-light district?

All of the beautiful Victorian mansions and pleasure halls of Storyville have been demolished. The infamous House of the Rising Sun's location has been forgotten over the years (indeed, if it ever really existed at all). But a townhouse at the top of the French Quarter still stands, and locals remember it as the brothel of Norma Wallace, the Last Madam of New Orleans and queen of the illicit sex industry for more than forty years.

Norma began working as a teenage street-walker in 1915, when the legal red-light district known as Storyville still existed. Though Storyville was closed down in 1917, the industry continued to thrive illegally; by 1920, Norma became the madam of her own bordello. She would continue to operate bordellos in the French Quarter for the next forty-two years, becoming the most powerful woman in the city's underworld. For four decades, her clients were governors, gangsters, and celebrities, affording "Queen" Norma all the protection she needed.

In 1936, Norma managed to accomplish what the police and FBI could not: she set up and arranged for the capture of Alvin Karpas, the most-wanted bank robber of the time. Karpas, of course, had been a customer at Norma's brothel.

A Storyville prostitute from the turn of the twentieth century, photographed by E.J. Bellocq.

The lion's share of that time would be spent in her townhouse/bordello at 1026 Conti Street. Norma and her girls opened up shop at this location in 1938, and it remained a lavish, politically protected house of prostitution until Norma's first arrest (and subsequent retirement from the underworld) in 1962. The building itself had almost as much connection to the sex trade as Norma did—it had once belonged to E.J. Bellocq, a local photographer most remembered for his photographs of Storyville prostitutes at the turn of the century.

After significant damage during Hurricane Katrina, the townhouse was painstakingly restored with many features left intact, including the door to the "hideout" where girls would hide during raids, the secret section of wall where Norma hid her money, and the red side door where payoffs were made.

THE LAST MADAM'S TOWNHOUSE

What: A historic and infamous brothel, restored (at least architecturally!) after Katrina

Where: 1026 Conti St. in the French Quarter

Cost: Usually closed to the public, as the rooms have been converted into condos

Pro Tip: Though many of the brothel's unique architectural features are hidden inside the building, explorers can still find the side door where police and informants were paid out along the right-hand side of the building (by the parking lot).

A SERENDIPITOUS STROKE OF THE PEN

How did an Irishman's poor handwriting turn into his lasting legacy?

Although the Cabildo museum focuses on New Orleans history, it features one item that was created in New Orleans but is used both in America and around the world today. It's a symbol that is to a certain extent "invisible in plain sight"—the American dollar sign.

During the Revolutionary War, America needed financial backing in order to fund their wartime needs. They looked to other countries for financial help but one philanthropist in particular was single-handedly the most helpful and in the process, left a symbol for currency that people now use on a daily basis.

Oliver Pollock, an Irish merchant, donated a huge portion of his fortune to the fledgling American government to help with their separation from England. He foresaw that this revolt would forever be remembered in history, so he wanted to be a part of this lasting legacy. He donated the equivalent of one billion of today's American dollars. But of course, at that time the accepted currency couldn't have been American money. Instead, the transaction was made with currency widely in use

---

The only physical acknowledgement of Oliver Pollock and his contribution to America is a small plaque on Chartres St. between St. Louis and Toulouse streets.

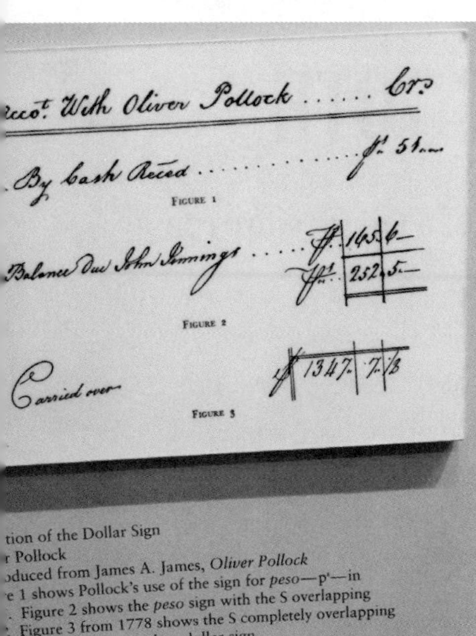

The creation of the dollar sign, and Oliver Pollock's penmanship.

POLLOCK'S DOLLAR SIGN

What: The American dollar sign

Where: Cabildo museum, 701 Chartres St.

Cost: $6

Pro Tip: During a visit to the Cabildo, ask a docent to show you where the Pollock artifacts are as they might have been moved to make room for temporary exhibits.

in the South and all of the Caribbean: the Spanish peso. Correspondence between Pollock and the new American leaders made numerous mentions of his donation of about 300,000 Spanish pesos. In order to save time, in his writings he began to simply abbreviate Spanish "peso" with a simple "ps." Pollock didn't have the best handwriting in the world, and over time the two letters moved closer and closer together. At one point his *p* overlapped his *s*, and the American dollar sign was born. The Cabildo museum on Jackson Square showcases some of Pollock's writings where one can clearly see the progression of the overlapping letters evolving into the dollar sign we use today.

NAMING THE SOUTH

How did the mispronunciation of a French word come to describe the South?

While the words "Dixie" and "Dixieland" are common in today's vernacular to refer to southern states, few of us wonder where the terms come from. There are many theories on the origin of the word "Dixie," ranging from it being named after Jeremiah Dixon of Mason-Dixon Line fame to Johan Dixie, a slave owner in Manhattan. One theory that many New Orleanians accept comes from the French Quarter. Located on the corner of Royal and Iberville streets is a Walgreens that many years ago was a bank where paper money was printed from 1835 to 1924. At this time in history, Louisiana had its own currency so people arriving in the state would need to convert their money to money they could use in Louisiana. One note that was quite common was the $10 bill. Although the state was American and the official language English, the people of the French Quarter still only spoke French. Because of this, the $10 note was printed with English on one side and French on the other. The French word for ten is *dix*, pronounced "dees." While locals pronounced it correctly, Americans arriving would often pronounce the

---

The site of the bank that printed the "Dix" note is today a Walgreens. It is located on the corner of Iberville and Royal streets. Visitors should look closely at the plaque just outside the entrance to the store as it describes the "birthplace of Dixie" as starting on that corner.

The "Dix" note. Notice how one side is in French.

The Birthplace of
"DIXIE"

On this site from 1835 to 1924 stood the Citizens State Bank, originator of the "Dixie." In its early days, the bank issued its own $10 bank note, with the French word "Dix" for "ten" printed on the note's face. As this currency became widespread, people referred to its place of origin as "the land of the Dix," which was eventually shortened to "Dixieland." Through song and legend, the word became synonymous with America's Southland.

Top: The James H. Cohen Antique Guns & Swords store, where the original dix *note can often be found.*
Bottom: Plaque commemorating the bank that once stood where the Walgreens is now and where the "Dix" note was printed.

BIRTHPLACE OF DIXIE PLAQUE

What: The origin of Dixieland

Where: 134 Royal St.

Cost: Free

Pro Tip: The James H. Cohen Antique Guns & Swords shop located at 437 Royal St. often has antique "dixies" on display (and for sale) for those wishing to see the actual bill.

word "dicks." The note quickly became known as a "dixie," and hence the land where the dixie was accepted was called "Dixieland." Visiting 134 Royal Street, one can find a plaque just outside the entrance of the Walgreens explaining this version of the origin of the word "Dixie" and how it was derived from the mispronunciation of the French word *dix*.

THE MOST FAMOUS OYSTER

What is (or isn't) Oysters Rockefeller?

It was 1889 and Jules Alciatore was at the helm of the then up-and-coming Antoine's Restaurant on St. Louis Street in the French Quarter. Although it was his father who started the restaurant in 1840, it was Jules who created THE dish that thrust the restaurant into stardom—Oysters Rockefeller.

The dish was invented out of necessity. People loved going to Antoine's for their classy escargot, and there was a shortage of the coveted snails. Jules took the challenge and turned to the oyster. He threw together butter, a variety of greens, and bread crumbs; then baked it. The result wowed his patrons! It was said that it was as rich as Rockefeller's wealth, hence the name. Because Oysters Rockefeller was such a hit, the recipe has been kept a secret to this day. While only a small handful of people know the true recipe, many people have tried to replicate it on their own. Because of this, the world believes that the primary ingredient is spinach. Amazingly, they're wrong. Although the recipe is still a tightly held secret, the family DID disclose one small fact: there is no spinach in the cocktail of greens that makes up Oysters Rockefeller!

Diners wishing to try another of Antoine's creations should order some Pommes de Terre Soufflees, which are fried puffed potatoes. They are a favorite among locals.

The original Oysters Rockefeller at Antoine's Restaurant. Courtesy Antoine's Restaurant.

ANOTINE'S OYSTER CREATION

What: Oysters Rockefeller

Where: Antoine's Restaurant

Cost: $15

Pro Tip: Get the Oyster Trio and try three oyster dishes: Oysters Rockefeller, Oysters Bienville, and Oysters Thermador!

AWASH IN HISTORY

Where can you literally bathe like an Emperor?

Napoleon Bonaparte just wanted to take a bath in peace.

One could hardly blame the First Consul of France for wanting a little quiet. Outside his private chambers, he was planning war with England, losing his Haitian colony in the Caribbean to slave rebellions, and short on funds. However, on this particular day in the spring of 1803, the leader was in high spirits. The new American government had approached the French, interested in purchasing the city of New Orleans. Napoleon instead decided to offer them the Louisiana territory, surmising that a quick sale would fund his European endeavors while at the same time divesting himself of those troublesome colonies across the Atlantic Ocean.

Relaxing in a hand-carved marble bathtub in the Tuileries, Napoleon was soon interrupted by his brothers, Joseph and Lucien, who were vehemently opposed to the sale. As the three men argued, Napoleon grew angry, eventually standing up in the bathtub to chastise his brothers. "There will be no debate!" he declared, reminding Joseph and Lucien that his word was final. When Joseph continued to argue, Napoleon fell back into the tub and propelled a wave of bathwater out of the marble

---

Want to see more of Napoleon? His death mask rests in the Cabildo, one of two Louisiana state museums in Jackson Square in the French Quarter.

A bathroom fit for a king. If Napoleon's marble tub is too small for you (the man was short, after all!), there's a full walk-in shower in the same bathroom, and you can still feel like royalty when using the gold fixtures!

THE EMPEROR'S BATHTUB

What: The bathtub where Napoleon allegedly decided the Louisiana Purchase

Where: Le Pavillon Hotel, 833 Poydras St., Napoleon Suite (Room 730)

Cost: While the hotel is free to enter, bathing in the tub will require spending the night in the Napoleon Suite. As you might imagine, the accommodations are priced for an emperor: most evenings start at $799/night!

Pro Tip: The suite boasts a few other notable antiques: the fireplace is from MacMillan castle in Scotland and is worth another $150,000, and two golden bowls also grace the same bathroom!

tub, soaking his brother. The argument was over.

But what happened to the bathtub in which the largest real estate deal in human history was decided? In 2006, it wound up in New Orleans.

While the Le Pavillon Hotel boasts $2.5 million in antiques and historic artifacts, their crown jewel is that same marble tub, which the hotel purchased for $350,000. It now sits in the bathroom of the appropriately named Napoleon Suite, a nod to one of the city's oddest acquisitions and an opportunity for visitors to literally immerse themselves in history and bathwater—simultaneously.

THROUGH THE PERLEY GATES

Where can you ride the oldest-running passenger rail line in the world?

The St. Charles Streetcar line first began operation on September 26, 1835. Its 6.5-mile path connected Canal Street and downtown New Orleans to the suburbs of Lafayette (now the Garden District) and Carrollton, both of which were annexed into New Orleans shortly after. The first cars ran on steam engines that produced soot and were quite noisy. Taking a step backward technologically, the steam engines were replaced by much quieter and cleaner horse and mule power. The streetcars eventually became electric on February 1, 1893.

In the early 1900s, New Orleans Public Service, Inc. (NOPSI) took over the streetcar system to provide more comfortable and consistent service. NOPSI commissioned Perley A. Thomas Car Works to manufacture new streetcars for the city in 1923. Perley streetcars gained international fame in Tennessee Williams's iconic *A Streetcar Named Desire*, which was written in 1947 and adapted to the silver screen in 1951. As fate would have it, the Desire Streetcar line, which ran on Bourbon Street as well as its namesake street, ceased operation in 1948, the same year the play premiered on Broadway.

As a true piece of Americana, the St. Charles Streetcar line became a National Historic Landmark in 2014.

A Perley streetcar. Note the original mahogany seats, brass fittings, and exposed light bulbs.

ORIGINAL PERLEY STREETCAR

What: New Orleans historic streetcars

Where: Along St. Charles Ave., from Canal St. to Carrollton St.

Cost: $1.25 ($0.40 for seniors). Daily and weekly passes also available.

Pro Tip: The last stop on the St. Charles Streetcar when heading back to the French Quarter is on the river side of Carondolet Street at Canal Street. Because nearly everyone exits the car at this stop, it is the best place to get on if you wish to go out to the Garden District/Carrollton/Uptown area. Most people will wait at the Common and St. Charles stop, so there is often a line and some people may have to wait for the next car. If paying cash, exact ticket cost is not required, but change will be given as an RTA voucher. The RTA GoMobile app is very convenient, has the latest schedule information, and allows for electronic ticket purchase.

Of the city's seventy-three original Perley streetcars, almost half are still running on the St. Charles line. The route's olive-and-crimson cars continue to boast the original mahogany seats, brass fittings, and exposed light bulbs. The New Orleans Regional Transit Authority, which took over the route in 1983, employs skilled craftsmen to machine parts for these antiques.

A streetcar ride on St. Charles is a uniquely New Orleans experience. The *clickety-clack* of the rails and the floral-scented breeze that wafts in through the old windows provides the perfect backdrop for admiring the Greek revival mansions and gorgeous oaks and magnolias along the avenue.

AN RX FOR HISTORY

Why is there a pharmacy museum in New Orleans?

Tucked into a small storefront in the heart of the French Quarter is a museum that is much more interesting on the inside than it might sound by name. The Pharmacy Museum is a treasure trove of early medicine, and it contains enough oddities that everyone seems to find something of note. It houses early pharmacy remedies such as leeches, prescriptions for whiskey during Prohibition, an authentic 1800s prescription file book, opium, and a seemingly ancient pharmacy counter, complete with countless tincture and medicine bottles.

But that is just the start. Exploring further, one will find authentic Voodoo powders and potions and an antique soda fountain that still works, although its lead pipes prevent it from being used. Additional exhibits include early surgical instruments, midwifery, and a rather extensive eyeglass collection that spans centuries. One of the more horrific presentations is of otolaryngology, with diagrams illustrating how to graft a new nose for those who lost theirs due to syphilis. Methods depicted include grafting a patient's middle finger onto his face to regrow

---

In 1804, Louisiana governor William C.C. Claiborne created a panel of physicians and pharmacists to administer the first three-hour oral licensing examination at the Cabildo in Jackson Square. The purpose was to ensure that those dispensing medicines had proper knowledge to do so.

Countless bottles can be viewed with various medicines and powders.

the skin, then later cutting the finger away. The Italian method shows how to attach a man's bicep skin to his face, keeping his arm bandaged to his head for several weeks until the new skin could be cut and reshaped into a nose.

But why is there a pharmacy museum in New Orleans? Louisiana became the first state to require licensing for many medical professions. The building that houses the museum was built in 1823 as the home and apothecary for Louis Dufilho, Jr., the first person to pass the Pharmacy Board in the United States and open a licensed drug store.

PHARMACY MUSEUM

What: A museum housed on the site of America's first licensed pharmacy

Where: 514 Chartres St.

Cost: $5 Admission ($4 students and seniors, free for children under 6). Open Tuesday–Saturday, 10 a.m.–4 p.m. The museum offers guided tours (included with admission) weekdays at 1 p.m.

Pro Tip: This Creole townhouse has a hidden, short-ceilinged second story called an entresol that was used for storage. From the front of the building, the tall, arched windows appear to be part of the first floor. Look into the carriageway and about halfway back in the ceiling you will see a hatch; that hatch was used to lift inventory from the delivery carriage straight up into the second floor storage area, which is where the arched windows are. The second owner, Dr. Dupas, is recounted in many ghost stories as using the hatch for much more sinister purposes, but there appears to be no evidence to support this tale.

YOU'LL PAY FOR THE WHOLE SEAT, BUT...

What was the "War of the Pews," and why was it so important?

Though the *Code Noir* of the 1700s mandated that all enslaved peoples should be Catholic, in reality the white aristocracy of New Orleans had no interest in attending Mass with those they considered property. The imposition of pew fees—a small monetary payment that earned a parishioner a place to sit while attending Mass—effectively barred the enslaved from the local churches.

In the 1830s, however, residents of the Tremé neighborhood decided to build a parish church of their own. Because Tremé had been settled by free people of color (the neighborhood is considered the oldest African American community in the country), the new Saint Augustine Church would be available to any who wished to worship within its walls. Upon hearing that pews were available to be purchased by people of color, opponents within the white communities began a campaign to buy all the pews in the new church beforehand to preserve the status quo. Thus, the "War

SAINT AUGUSTINE CHURCH

What: The oldest integrated Catholic community in America

Where: 1210 Governor Nicholls St.

Cost: Free

Pro Tip: Though Mass is held at 5 p.m. on Wednesdays, only the 10 a.m. Sunday Mass has the full Saint Augustine Jazz Choir!

Humble but resolute. Unassuming yet deeply spiritual and historically important. What can be said about Saint Augustine could also be said of the Tremé community, currently struggling with issues of gentrification and historic/cultural preservation in a rapidly growing—and changing—neighborhood.

of the Pews" commenced, and a brief but strange cultural conflict played out in the new parish.

Happily, the war was eventually won by the free people of color, who bought three times the number of pews as their antagonists. They then went on to purchase the pews along both aisles and immediately donated them for use by slaves. This unimaginably progressive move meant that by its opening in 1842, Saint Augustine had the most integrated congregation of any church in the United States.

Today, Saint Augustine stands as the oldest African American Catholic parish in the nation. Narrowly avoiding closure following Hurricane Katrina, the community again rallied to save their beloved church, even going so far as to barricade themselves in the rectory until a compromise was secured. In March 2009, the church announced it would not be closing, and Mass continues to be held weekly.

If you visit during the Lenten season (the forty days before Easter each year), stop by to see if Saint Augustine is holding its annual Fish Fry Friday, a favorite among the local Catholic communities and soul food lovers alike!

A MIRACULOUS GRAVEYARD

What do the sick hope to find in Saint Roch's Chapel?

While New Orleans is home to many impressive churches, one less-visited chapel tucked into one of the city's residential neighborhoods has been known for its miraculous tendencies since its inception 150 years ago.

In 1867, as yet another yellow fever epidemic raged throughout the city, a German priest, Reverend Peter Leonard Thevis, prayed for his parishioners. Turning to Saint Roch (the Catholic saint often invoked against plagues in the Middle Ages), Reverend Thevis swore that if his parish was spared from the epidemic, he would build a chapel in the saint's honor.

When no one in the Holy Trinity parish died from the fever (and, in fact, were spared from yet another epidemic a decade later), the Reverend was as good as his word and built a chapel, shrine, and cemetery all dedicated to the Saint who had miraculously protected his congregation.

Since then, many sick and injured residents have made pilgrimages to the fabled chapel asking Saint Roch for

---

When Saint Roch was dying from the plague, he was (allegedly) miraculously healed after a dog brought him loaves of bread and licked his wounds each day. This loyal pooch remained at Roch's side until the day he died, and Saint Roch is now also the patron saint of dogs as a result.

Eagle-eyed readers might have noticed the stained-glass windows are missing in this photo of the chapel. The entire chapel is currently undergoing extensive renovation but is scheduled to be completed by summer 2020.

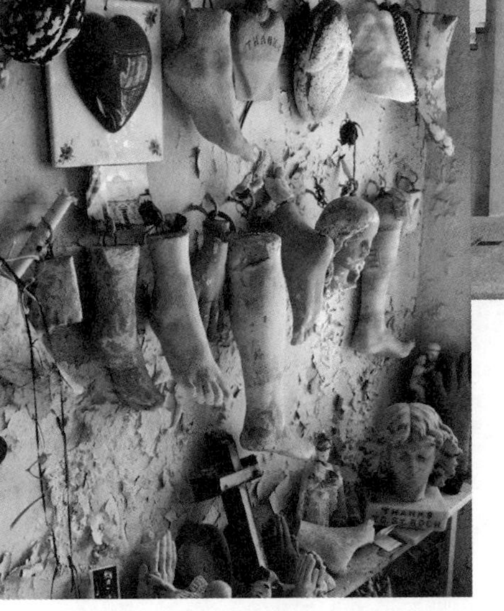

Prosthetic limbs, crutches, and braces line both walls of the chapel along with tokens of thanks and prayer candles. If you arrive and the chapel is unexpectedly closed, this room can still be spied by looking through the barred window on the right-hand side of the chapel.

SAINT ROCH'S CHAPEL

What: A shrine where locals pray for miraculous cures since the 1800s

Where: Saint Roch Cemetery #1, 1725 St. Roch Ave.

Cost: Free

Pro Tip: The cemetery closes at 4 p.m., so plan accordingly. The Saint Roch Market, six blocks away, offers great lunch options.

a miracle cure of their personal afflictions. The shrine itself overflows with relics of those same prayers: prosthetic limbs, crutches, flowers, candles, and other items left behind by both the hopeful and those who return to thank Saint Roch for their own personal miracles.

DON'T FEAR THE REAPER

Is there a religion in New Orleans even stranger than Voodoo?

In a city where even Voodoo is commonplace, locals don't tend to bat an eye at strange religious practices. Steven Bragg built the exception to that rule.

Not long after Hurricane Katrina, Bragg dreamt of a robed skeleton holding a scythe. In an unmistakably female voice, the skeleton told him that if he would build her a shrine, she would protect his home in return. Bragg didn't recognize the figure but built the shrine anyway. Its first iteration was a simple, white-robed skeleton inside a shed in Bragg's backyard.

But strange rumors fly fast in New Orleans, and soon Bragg found that members of the Latino community were visiting the shrine to leave tequila, roses, and cigarettes. Bragg may not have recognized the figure, but others did: La Santisima Muerte had come to Louisiana.

Originally a Mexican phenomenon, Santisima Muerte (literally Saint Death)

THE THREE REAPERS

What: A shrine to the Mexican folk saint, La Santisima Muerte

Where: Spiritual supply shop Botanica Macumba, 3154 Saint Claude Ave.

Cost: Free to enter and view the shrine. The Botanica is open Tuesday through Sunday, 11 a.m.–7 p.m.

Pro Tip: It's not just Santisima Muerte who has a home at the Botanica. You'll also find shrines and altars dedicated to Voodoo, Vodou, Lucumi/Santeria, and several other esoteric practices.

The newest incarnation of the altar boasts not one, but three reapers: The white-robed reaper, representing purity; the red-robed reaper, representing love and passion; and the black-robed reaper, representing the underworld, darkness, and protection from evil.

is a Mexican folk saint whose veneration has spread across the continent. Religious studies scholar Andrew Chestnut estimates that ten to twelve million followers of this "skeleton saint" exist in North America. Like Voodoo, Santisima Muerte has gained notoriety thanks to Hollywood exaggerations (the practice makes an appearance in the series *Breaking Bad*) and others' misconceptions.

Take, for instance, the association with Mexican cartels seen on television. Because death comes for us all, Chestnut explains, "She's the saint who doesn't discriminate, so she accepts all comers: LGBT, prostitutes, narcos." He acknowledges that there are criminals who pray to her: "However, most of her devotees on both sides of the border are not narcos." Indeed, a town like New Orleans—well known for accepting those from all walks of life—seems a perfect fit.

Bragg's shrine has since moved indoors to newly launched Botanica Macumba and is open to any who wish to learn more about this strange addition to local spirituality.

Though Bragg's shrine was the first to be prominently featured in the city, the imagery (and followers!) of Santisima Muerte continue to spread throughout the city. Another statue of the folk saint can now be seen in the New Orleans Healing Center, very near the International Shrine of Marie Laveau (see page 120).

SHAKEN, NOT STIRRED

What's the Drink We Hate to Love?

There is one phrase guaranteed to get you banned from a bar in New Orleans: "Ten Ramos Gin Fizzes, please."

Think of the Ramos Gin Fizz as the New Orleans breakfast smoothie of the late 1800s: fresh lemon and lime juice, orange flower water, egg white, half-and-half, sweet gin, simple syrup, ice, and club soda. It was popularized by businessmen as a quick, mid-morning break from the office.

It sounds simple enough, so why the controversy? The answer lies in the preparation. Maintaining fresh eggs at a bar in summertime is tricky. There is also no major producer of quality orange flower water, which means each bar needs to make it in-house. The straw that broke the camel's back (or in this case, the bartender's shoulder) is the amount of shaking involved to get the cream and egg to emulsify and create the perfect egg foam consistency.

Henry Charles "Carl" Ramos invented the drink in 1888 at his bar, the Imperial Cabinet, located on Gravier at Carondolet in the American Sector. He employed twenty "shaker boys" to provide the muscle required to make the drink properly, which reports show took six to eleven

---

In a fun twist of fate, Mary's Ace Hardware store on Rampart Street, located in what was once Ramos's residence, placed their paint section in what would have been Ramos's own living room.

At his bar, Henry Ramos employed up to thirty-three people at a time. While it is not documented, Ramos said one of his shakers was young Charles Ponzi, who went on to invent the Ponzi scheme.

minutes of shaking. He also owned perhaps the country's largest hennery to provide the 5,000 eggs he used weekly!

Bartenders today spend roughly one minute shaking the drink. It is a long sixty seconds, especially considering that the martini tin is ice-cold to the touch. Those wishing to try a six-minute version can head to the Bourbon O Bar, where famous bartender Cheryl Charming retrofitted a bubble tea shaker to fit a martini tin. The best part? It is very reminiscent of a paint can shaker, which is the business Ramos went into during Prohibition. In fact, the paint section of Mary's Ace Hardware at 732 North Rampart Street was once the front room of Carl Ramos's own residence.

RAMOS GIN FIZZ

What: A delicious cocktail that can be drunk any time of day but is especially popular in the morning

Where: The Sazerac Bar inside the Roosevelt Hotel, 130 Roosevelt Way

Bourbon O Bar, 730 Bourbon St.

Cost: $$

Pro Tip: Go during slower times to really appreciate the experience and be sure to watch how it is made and poured. Ask the bartender at the Bourbon O Bar about the drink's history and prompt the person behind the Sazerac Bar to tell you why theirs is famous.

SIDEWALK BUFFET

Wasting away again...on Bourbon Street?

Long before there were Parrotheads, Jimmy Buffet was just a college freshman trying to meet girls. He saw his Sigma Pi fraternity brother use a guitar to attract coeds in 1965, so he asked for lessons. It worked so well that he failed out of school in 1966. He re-enrolled in Pearl River Junior College to keep out of the Vietnam draft and started commuting from Poplarville, Mississippi, eighty miles each way to busk in the French Quarter for income.

Starting in 1966 and lasting for three years, he set up by Decatur between Toulouse and St. Phillip, outside two bars where Bob Dylan himself had spent Mardi Gras just two years prior. The area's more Bohemian crowd appreciated Jimmy's folk style and protest tunes. In 1967, Jimmy and his friends got their first recurring gig playing cover tunes at tiny Trader John's, located next to present-day Preservation Hall. But his big break was at the Bayou Room Tavern on Bourbon Street, where all the young bands wanted to play. After the bar's own band members were tragically killed in a car crash on the Causeway Bridge—the very bridge Jimmy drove back-and-forth to school—he was hired to play Tuesday through Sunday nights.

MARGARITAVILLE

What: Jimmy Buffet's first performance spots

Where: At his busking spots on Decatur at Toulouse, outside 515 St. Phillip, and what would be 734 St. Peter (Trader John's).

Cost: Free

Pro Tip: Grab a margarita in a go cup in order to toast the legend properly!

Parrotheads can pilgrimage to one of the spots where it all began, at the corner of Toulouse and Decatur.

Because Jimmy Buffet has a long history and ingrained love for New Orleans (and vice versa), he was selected as a subject for the Jazz Fest poster in 2011. He is depicted on a corner where he played—Conti at Chartres streets—with his Falcon parked nearby and his younger self in the background glancing over his shoulder at what he would someday become.

Jimmy graduated with a B.S. in history from the University of Southern Mississippi in 1969. He married, moved to Nashville, and cut his first record in 1970. By 1973, he was already living in Key West, Florida, and gaining fans. His musical *Escape to Margaritaville* premiered at the Saenger Theater in 2017 before opening on Broadway. It was only fitting, since the Saenger is where he first got the notion to become a performer at just twelve years old; his uncle had had an office there and supplied the boy with free balcony passes for shows.

The annual New Orleans Jazz Fest poster is the largest grossing festival poster in the world.

SIGN OF THE TIMES

Where can you literally see "change"?

The Omni Royal Orleans Hotel lies in the heart of the French Quarter. The first hotel built on that footprint was the luxurious Saint Louis Hotel. Rather plain on the outside, the hotel was known for a stunning interior, capped off with its notable rotunda. The resort was constructed between 1835 and 1838 for $1.5 million ($44 million in today's money) and housed grand ballrooms and beautiful dining salons in addition to the city's auction exchange, complete with slave block.

The resort burned down in 1841 but was rebuilt even larger and grander than before under the design of Joseph Isadore de Pouilly, the same Frenchman who designed the first. Renamed Saint Louis Hotel & Exchange, every Saturday slave auctions took place inside the ornate rotunda. Trafficked humans were auctioned off to the backdrop of priceless artwork, games of billiards, and clinking cocktail glasses of the wealthy plantation and business owners.

The hotel was a destination in the South until it was captured and used as a hospital by the Union soldiers in 1862. Eventually abandoned and falling into neglect, the

---

The splendor of the Royal Orleans Hotel inspired the Led Zeppelin song "Royal Orleans" and author Arthur Hailey's book *Hotel*, which later became a major, award-winning television series of the same name directed by Aaron Spelling.

The original, darker arches of the St. Louis Hotel & Exchange are clearly distinguishable from the newer Omni Royal Hotel.

A drawing of the original St. Louis Hotel & Exchange displayed inside the Omni Royal Hotel.

hurricane of 1915 finished it off. Much of the rubble was removed and replaced by a parking lot.

The Royal Orleans arose in its place in 1960. Its façade was replicated from drawings of the original St. Louis Hotel, down to the exact stone archways and wrought iron railings. A section of the original St. Louis Hotel & Exchange sign and archways remain to this day as a reminder of the horrors that once took place on this site. Fittingly, there is one word from the faded, original sign that remains: CHANGE.

CHANGE

What: Remnants of the original structure

Where: Chartres Street side of the Omni Royal Orleans Hotel, across the street from Napoleon House and Hotel St. Helene at 504 and 508 Chartres St.

Cost: Free

Pro Tip: Step into the main entrance of the Omni Royal Orleans Hotel on St. Louis Street and go up the staircase and toward the concierge desk to view a drawing of the original St. Louis Hotel & Exchange.

AMERICA'S FRIENDS TO THE SOUTH

Why is there a statue of Simon Bolivar in NOLA?

Near the corner of Basin and Canal streets sits a statue in disrepair dedicated to Simon Bolivar. The question that few can answer is: why? There is no documentation of Bolivar's living or even visiting New Orleans, so why the memorial?

It was November 1957 when then-mayor Chep Morrison decided to recognize the port of New Orleans as the North American link to our South American neighbors. It was a move to emphasize the fact that countries of the north and south can live in harmony. The Bolivarian Society of America, with representatives from Venezuela, Columbia, Ecuador, Bolivia, Peru, and Panama, agreed. The country of Venezuela sent a gift of a statue of Simon Bolivar "the Liberator" who led the six aforementioned countries to their independence. The event included a parade and speeches made by the mayor as well as by the members of the Bolivarian Society of America. Flag poles were erected, and the flags of each Bolivarian country plus that of the United States were raised while the national anthem of each country was played.

Sadly, today it's only a shell of its former self. It stands as a memory of a day when the United States' relationship with its neighbors to the south was celebrated.

Other historic sites to visit on Basin Street are the Vietnam Memorial and the Benito Juarez statue.

Simon Bolivar statue at the corner of Basin and Canal streets.

THE SOUTH AMERICAN LIBERATOR

What: Simon Bolivar statue

Where: Basin St. at Canal St.

Cost: Free

Pro Tip: Continue on Basin St. and cross Canal Street to see the Molly Marine statue. Unveiled in 1943, this is the first statue of a woman Marine in the United States.

SINGING OAK

Where can you hear a symphony of wind chimes?

New Orleans is known as The Crescent City, The Big Easy, and The City That Care Forgot. No place better exemplifies the latter two than a special tree in City Park.

A shady spot under the branches of a sprawling, centuries-old Southern live oak tree is a welcoming respite from a sultry Louisiana day. One particular tree, lovingly dubbed the Singing Oak, offers not only a cool shelter to rest under, but also an enchanting lullaby.

The Chime Tree was designed by Jim Hart in 1948. It is filled with various sizes of wind chimes that range up to fourteen feet in length. The aluminum alloy tubes are all set to the pentatonic scale, thereby ringing the same five notes per octave. A sign at the base of the tree notes, "This is the same scale used in West African music, gospel music, and New Orleans jazz."

The tree is visible to all those who pass by, but the chimes making this melodic—even magical—experience are artfully arranged so as to be hidden in plain sight. The wind chimes have been placed in the foliage interior and painted black to blend in with the surrounding branches, making them easily missed by the casual observer. To find the tree, go to the southeast shore of Big Lake (this is near the Esplanade main entrance). The Zemurray paved

---

Sitting under the expansive shade tree with its soothing, nature-created music of wind chimes is the perfect place for peaceful meditation.

The Singing Oak.

walking path will be on the right and left as you look across the meadow. Walk straight through the meadow, directly between the two paths and look for a large, lone oak tree (often there is a bench or two beneath it). You should also see the small dedication sign about twenty feet from the ancient trunk. Sit for a moment and feel the enchantment and nurturing sounds of nature.

THE CHIME TREE

What: A tree that sings

Where: City Park Zemurray Trail, just southeast of Big Lake

Cost: Free

Pro Tip: There is another piece of tree art nearby. From the Singing Oak, leave the park and walk along the south side of Bayou St. John on Moss Street. Cross the bayou on picturesque, wood-planked Magnolia Bridge, and continue south on Moss Street (turns into Jefferson Davis Parkway) toward Orleans Avenue. Just past Orleans, look to the left and see a dead tree trunk (lost in a hurricane) that has been beautifully carved into birds, guitars, a keyboard, and other local iconography by chainsaw artist Marlin Miller. If you feel the need for a meal or a snack after viewing, continue a bit farther down the Parkway as you are right near many fantastic, Mid-City neighborhood restaurants!

DIVE INTO CHRISTMAS

What the hell is a possum drop, and *why* would you ever drink one?

To the average tourist, it looks like an abandoned shack—decaying, rusted, and threatening to fall apart at the first stiff breeze. The red lights both inside and out give it the impression of a horror movie set. Anthony Bourdain once called it a "national treasure," but to the regulars, it's just "Snake's" (a shortening of the longer, official Snake & Jake's Christmas Club Lounge). The perennial favorite dive bar in a town chock full of them, the bar's legend is built more on its stories than anything else, and everyone who's ever visited seems to have one.

Belly up to the bar and you might hear about "naked night," when a group of fraternity brothers showed up to the bar naked, having heard you could get a free drink that way (tip: you can't). The bartender kicked them out, and peace was momentarily restored—until the guys realized they'd locked their keys in their car. They

THE DIVE TO END ALL DIVES

What: Snake & Jake's Christmas Club Lounge and its "only in New Orleans" specialty drink

Where: To quote the bar website: "We are located at 7612 Oak St, at Hillary, in between Broadway and Carrollton. There is a lighted wreath in front. Good luck."

Cost: Beer for $2, well cocktails during happy hour for $3

Pro Tip: The bar opens every day at 7 p.m. and happy hour runs until 10 p.m. Though the bar officially stays open until 7 a.m., in truth the bar closes "when everybody's done drinking."

There's no sign. No address. Just that wreath—and good luck figuring out how long that's been there. This picture was also taken during the day; it's harder to find at night, but sometimes that's part of the fun, right?

wound up throwing a brick through the car's window just to make their embarrassing escape. You might meet one of the regulars who spent an entire evening unknowingly drinking with George Clooney (the bar was literally too dark to recognize the A-list actor).

One of the bar's most famous stories is immortalized in its "signature cocktail," the Possum Drop. It's exactly the kind of concoction you'd expect from the environment—a shot of Jagermeister dropped into a pint of Schlitz (which tastes surprisingly like root beer). According to its creator, the night the drink was invented, a possum literally fell through the roof and onto the shoulders of the bartender. There are countless "you should have been there" stories told nightly, ranging from the tame to the absolutely unrepeatable. Ask the regulars. Ask the bartenders.

Just remember to keep an eye on the ceiling.

When the bar's lighting or atmosphere becomes too claustrophobic, locals escape to the courtyard in the back, prominently decorated year-round with—what else?—plastic Christmas decorations.

BEING COOL IN NOLA

What's the best way to cool down in NOLA?

Many places have their own icy dessert. Philadelphia has water ice, Hawaii has shave ice, and New Orleans has the sno-ball. New Orleans's very own ice treat has been a favorite since the 1930s. At its basic level, it is nothing more than shaved ice with a syrup flavoring poured over the top. Of course, New Orleans can't leave well enough alone. Sno-balls can be found topped with condensed milk, candy, or fruit to name just a few things. They can also be found stuffed with soft serve ice cream or even cheesecake!

Back in the '30s, George Ortolano and Ernest Hansen independently came up with a motorized machine that could shave ice. While Ortolano marketed his machine for others to use in their own sno-ball businesses, Hansen created a sno-ball shop that's still in business today. Many locals believe that Hansen's on Tchoupitoulas Street is the very best place to stand in line for a sno-ball, but there are countless stands and shops to help patrons form their own opinions.

While the spring and summer months are the usual season for finding sno-balls, some places are open year-round.

Resist the urge to eat your sno-ball quickly to avoid brain freeze.

Hansen's is a local favorite.

SNO-BALLS IN NOLA

What: Super soft shaved ice flavored with a syrup and often topped with condensed milk and stuffed with ice cream

Where: Various sno-ball shops/stands in New Orleans

Cost: $2–$6

Pro Tip: Because sno-ball businesses are all independently owned and operated, they each have different hours and/or dates of operation. People often go in search of a certain sno-ball only to be greeted with a "Sorry we're closed" sign. Sno-ball seekers should definitely call ahead to verify operating times.

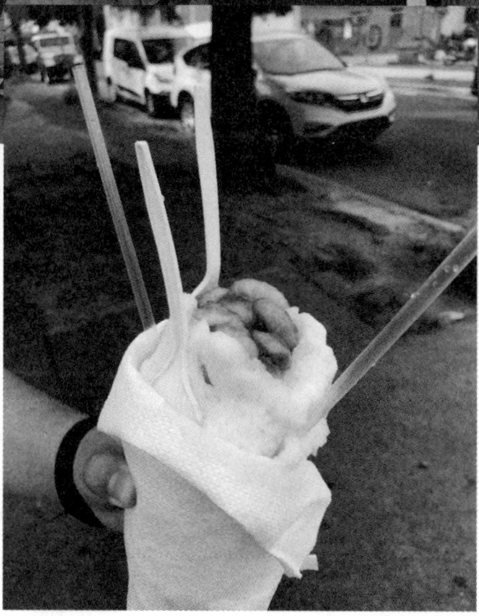

Bananas Foster sno-ball.

THE FIRST

Where can you eat food from the first Asian group to settle in the USA?

The Filipino population of New Orleans might be the "sleeper" of the immigrant groups. The relatively unknown community was first made public in an 1883 *Harper's Weekly* article written by Lafcadio Hearn, dating the arrival of these "ManilaMen" to 1843. Reports actually date the first Filipinos arriving as early as 1765 when runaway sailors, having escaped Spanish galleons sailing from the Spanish-occupied Philippines to the New World, sought refuge in the lush foliage along the southern coast of Lake Borgne. They established the village of Saint Malo. Eventually, they moved to Barataria and created "Little Manila," now known as Jean Lafitte in Jefferson Parish. Some residents can trace their heritage back eight generations to these original ManilaMen. The first official monument to Filipino-Americans in the United States lies in Jean Lafitte.

These hardworking, resourceful men not only utilized their fishing and net-making skills to catch shrimp, they also pioneered the practice of sun-drying shrimp in order to preserve them. Their packaged shrimp contained no added oils and were therefore safe to eat almost indefinitely, making them a lucrative trade product to

---

Everything is made to order, so a forty-five-minute wait for food is typical, but any adventurous eater looking for authenticity will find the flavors and experience well worth it!

Dinuguan (left) is like a pork stew thickened with pig's blood but without the typical tin-like flavor that most blood dishes contain, and Chicken Adobo (right). Rice accompanies every dish.

China via the shipping ports of New Orleans.

By the twentieth century, around 2,000 Filipinos urbanized to New Orleans, making it the center of the Filipino community in Louisiana. Most lived around Rampart Street between Elysian Fields and Esplanade. Today, in the back of a tiny corner store not far from the other end of Rampart, Chef Crispin Pasia serves up authentic Filipino dishes tasty enough to earn him the title as one of the Best Chefs in Louisiana in 2016 and 2019. Recruited by Chef Paul Prudhomme (and one of his main chefs for eighteen years), it is clear from the wall memorabilia that Chef Pasia still thinks the world of his former employer and friend. His food, however, is certainly authentic to his Filipino roots.

CK'S HOT SHOPPE

What: Authentic food from an overlooked Asian-Creole community

Where: 1433 Baronne St.

Cost: $$

Pro Tip: It is a tiny, hidden restaurant near the Southern Food and Beverage Museum (a great pre-dinner or post-lunch stop!), which is easily accessible via bicycle or car. Need help ordering? Ask award-winning Chef Pasia for advice. Shy? Here's a short list: Lumpia is like a Filipino eggroll, which is always a good place to start. *Adobo* and *pancit* are also good beginner dishes. And be sure to get the flan for dessert; it is larger and denser than Mexican flan and easily shareable.

THE RINK

Was it really used for ice skating in the 1880s?

The Rink building dates back to December 1884. The city was hastily preparing for the World's Industrial Cotton Centennial Exposition, which later became known as the first World's Fair. To capitalize on the event, Clara Hagan erected a large, barn-like wooden building with skylights to house an attraction: the Crescent City Skating Rink. Contrary to what many guidebooks and tour guides profess, this was not an ice-skating rink. The technology to make ice by running glycerin through copper pipes had been invented in 1876, but Hagan's structure was instead built for the enormously popular sport of roller-skating. Fair attendees flocked to Hagan's state-of-the-art facility to test out the recently added toe stop and the newly patented use of steel ball bearings that allowed for greater speed with little effort.

While roller-skating has endured beyond its 1880s heyday, The Rink itself was short-lived. In January 1889, it was converted into a stable to house three hundred horse stalls plus carriages. This was followed by a 1912 renovation

---

The building across Washington Street from The Rink was a well-known training facility in the 1880s for many prizefighters including John L. Sullivan and Jake Kilrain. The two went fist-to-fist in 1889 in the last bareknuckle heavyweight championship that lasted a walloping two hours and sixteen minutes through seventy-five rounds.

The floor today has been tiled for pedestrian shoppers and is the hub of commerce for the Garden District neighborhood.

into a mortuary. Eventually, the building became a Texaco gas station in the 1930s with a shoe repair shop and other little stores attached. By 1978, a *Times-Picayune* newspaper article stated that the once aesthetically appealing façade of the structure had become tattered and run-down, and the original structure had been lost due to haphazard and "tacky" additions.

The Rink was bought that same year. It underwent massive renovations to peel away the shabby veneers and resurrect the historic structure beneath. It opened in 1979 as a small shopping center. The Garden District Book Store—which has hosted numerous famous authors including native Anne Rice—and Still Perkin' Coffee Shop are local favorites.

THE RINK SHOPPING CENTER

What: Debunking a very popular myth

Where: 2727 Prytania St.

Cost: Free

Pro Tip: You will need a quarter to use the toilet here, or you can make a purchase at the coffee shop to use theirs. Take the St. Charles Streetcar to get here. If you arrive before 3 p.m., take a walk into the cemetery. Stop into Commander's Palace and get their Garden District self-walking tour brochure and lose yourself among the beautiful mansions on the neighboring streets.

A HOUSE FIT FOR A NUN

Where is the oldest building in the Mississippi River Valley?

In 1727, France sent over Ursuline nuns with the understanding that they were needed as teachers. The reality was that they were mostly needed to care for hospitalized patients. Seven years later, a convent was built for them at 1100 Chartres Street in the French Quarter, and that is where it still sits today. It's considered to be the oldest structure in New Orleans as well as the entire Mississippi River Valley, but the convent building we see today is not exactly what was built back in 1734. The first building wasn't built with New Orleans weather in mind, so in 1751 the convent was rebuilt and enlarged using more brick than wood to withstand New Orleans's humid climate. The building we see today was used as a convent, orphanage, school, and hospital over the years. Amazingly, it has survived various city-wide disasters, including the fires of 1788 and 1794 and hurricanes Camille, Betsy, and most recently Katrina. Today the Ursuline Convent is a museum where visitors can view a large collection of New Orleans

URSULINE CONVENT

What: One of the oldest buildings in the South

Where: 1100 Chartres St.

Cost: $8.00 General Admission, $7.00 Seniors, $6.00 Students/Military

Pro Tip: Be sure to see the Bible dated from 1515 printed in Nuremberg, Germany, sixty years after the invention of movable type. This Bible is two centuries older than the city of New Orleans and two years older than the Protestant Reformation!

Left: Ursuline Convent garden.
Bottom: Bible printed in 1515.

history covering the past three hundred years. In addition, many ghost tour guides stop in front and tell the vampire tale of the "Casket Girls," although there is no real validity to the story.

Andrew Jackson visited the Ursuline Convent to thank the nuns for their prayers during the Battle of New Orleans in 1815.

AN ELDER AMONG THE ANCIENTS

Where in New Orleans could you climb a tree to say hello to a giraffe?

Sometime in New Orleans's storied past (perhaps even before the founding of the city itself), a tiny acorn fell to the ground. Unseen and undisturbed, it rooted and began to grow. Over the centuries, as the city grew, that acorn metamorphosed into a mighty live oak tree that the locals now call the "Tree of Life." A favorite among the residents who know where to find it, the site has become a popular place for weddings, films, picnics, tree climbing (of course), and surprisingly exotic nature-watching.

While the tree is known to the locals as the Tree of Life, it's officially registered as the "Etienne de Boré Oak" (named after the first mayor of New Orleans who once owned the land where the tree stands as part of his plantation). A massive and majestic example of the Southern live oak species (*Quercus virginiana*), the tree measures around sixty feet in height (six to seven stories tall!), is thirty-four feet in circumference, and its branches spread to a crown more than 160 feet wide. Its age is much more mysterious: though a sign proclaims the tree was

---

The roots of the Tree of Life extend underground as far out as the branches do above you, explaining why the tree stands apart from all the others: there's no room for them to grow!

The enormous canopy of branches provides enough shade that underneath the boughs is a popular picnic and wedding spot, even in the hottest part of summer.

THE TREE OF LIFE

What: One of the largest live oak trees in New Orleans

Where: Audubon Park, East Dr., New Orleans

Cost: Free

Pro Tip: If you'd like to officially meet the giraffes, the Audubon Zoo next door is open 10 a.m.–5 p.m. Monday through Friday, and 10 a.m. - 6 p.m. on Saturday and Sunday ($19/adults, $14/children ages 2–12).

born in 1740, experts have weighed in claiming the tree's age could be anywhere from one hundred to more than five hundred years old.

Despite its beauty and magnificence, it's likely that what makes it the locals' favorite is its location: tucked into a quiet corner of Audubon Park, the city eventually built the local zoo next door. The tree is taller than the animals' enclosures, and brave explorers can climb up the tree and sometimes find themselves eye-to-eye with the giraffes that live just a few hundred feet away!

A TUNNEL RUNS THROUGH IT

How did citizens save the French Quarter?

The 1956 Federal-Aid Highway Act established high-speed roadways to connect all corners of the United States. The federal government provided a whopping 90 percent of the funds needed to erect the six-lane, elevated Interstate 10 through New Orleans, but it was not enough. The project was delayed until more federal funding could be secured to create an underground tunnel in order to ease traffic congestion in the Central Business District. Impatient, the city fronted the $1.3 million tunnel construction cost in 1964 in order to hit another deadline: the architecturally stunning Rivergate Exhibition Hall. Erected on top of the tunnel, the hall needed to be finished in time for the city's 250th birthday in 1968.

Tunnel compete, the city had the infrastructure and funding ready. But resident Martha Robinson's "Stop the Highwaymen" campaign was gaining momentum. The highway's construction meant that the French Quarter would lie directly under the concrete behemoth, leaving the neighborhood's color, vibrancy, and music lost to street noise and shadows. Historic buildings would be trampled

---

French Quarter advocate Martha Gilmore Robinson (1888–1981) was also a founding member of Le Petit Théâtre du Vieux Carré in 1916.

One end of the tunnel collapsed April 29, 2016, opening an enormous sinkhole at the foot of Canal Street (the tunnel culminates at Poydras Street).

RIVERGATE TUNNEL

What: A tunnel that lies forgotten beneath the downtown area

Where: Under Harrah's Casino, part of which is used for their valet parking

Cost: Valet parking charge

Pro Tip: Public access to the tunnel has been blocked, but a car dashboard camera and use of Harrah's Casino valet service can provide an inside look at a portion of it (just get permission to film first).

for construction. Politicians were ready to move forward, but the residents were not. Their cries received national support in 1966 when the usual boisterous photos from Mardi Gras printed in *Life* and *Time* magazines were replaced with morbid images of balconies draped in black and "Save the Death of the City" posters.

So how did the French Quarter get saved? The key was to make Jackson Square a historic landmark. Unable to construct within a protected area, the interstate plans were redrawn, and the French Quarter was spared. The tunnel, already constructed and paid for by the city, quite literally became a sunk cost. It is closed off to the public, but a section of it is currently used for Harrah's Casino valet parking.

IT CAN'T RAIN ALL THE TIME

How did a piece of graffiti become an icon to post-Katrina New Orleans?

In 2008, as Hurricane Gustav swept into the city, a mysterious figure arrived in New Orleans. Surreptitiously, under the cover of darkness and the approaching storm, the man went to work with stencils and spray paint. When he disappeared, fourteen original pieces of graffiti marked his passing. The British graffiti artist Banksy had made his mark—literally—on New Orleans.

Over a decade later, few of the pieces remain. Some have been painted over, others removed, and still others lost when the building that served as their canvas was demolished. But one still remains just a few blocks outside the French Quarter: officially christened *Nola*, it's more often known to the locals as the *Umbrella Girl*.

The imagery is both stark and poignant. A young girl, dressed in black, stands under an umbrella. If her expression seems confused, it's easy to understand why; the rain is pouring from inside her umbrella. In an interview later, Banksy said the art "represents how some of the

---

Another controversial Banksy piece painted at the same time depicted National Guardsmen as looters, with two uniformed men filling a shopping cart with electronic items. That piece can now be seen in the lobby of the International House Hotel on Camp Street.

When other graffiti artists started tagging the wall right next to their idol's work, building owners painted over all other graffiti and then covered the piece with plexiglass to protect it. The would-be thieves used that plexiglass as a guideline when they tried to cut the section of wall away; you can still see some of the damage caused by their circular saw on the left-hand side.

things that are supposed to protect us can also harm us." Residents still reeling from Hurricane Katrina could relate, as the town suffered most of its harm when the levees (designed specifically to protect the city from the storm) failed and the city was inundated with water.

That empathic bond may be what has protected the *Umbrella Girl* when so many of her contemporaries have disappeared. In 2014, a group of men attempted to remove the graffiti by literally chiseling away the piece of the wall that held her, only to flee when they were challenged and questioned by neighbors. Their motive seems obvious: other similar pieces have sold for hundreds of thousands of dollars.

But not the *Umbrella Girl*. She remains on her corner (now protected by plexiglass), still wondering if this rain will ever end.

NOLA, THE UMBRELLA GIRL

What: An original Banksy graffiti piece, still present after more than a decade

Where: The corner of North Rampart and Kerlerec Sts.

Cost: Free

Pro Tip: If you absolutely must have this art for your own home, no need for a hammer and chisel—the artist also produced a series of signed stencil-on-canvas prints. Replicas of the art can also be found online, at NOMA, and in T-shirt shops and tattoo parlors throughout town.

HONORING THE NAMELESS

How did one church in New Orleans commemorate countless "lost" souls?

For decades in the Tremé neighborhood, residents had been uncovering bones.

Developed on top of several eighteenth-century plantations, those living in America's oldest African American neighborhood were well aware that their houses and businesses were built—quite literally—on the bones of the enslaved. Remains uncovered during renovations or new construction often indicated unmarked slave graveyards or sites where these enslaved people were simply buried in shallow graves in the same fields they had worked.

In 2004, Saint Augustine Church decided to honor these countless souls who were buried without any funeral, last rites, or commemoration. A massive iron cross built from thick chain was laid on its side alongside the church's outer wall. Smaller chains and manacles (the sort worn by the enslaved throughout

THE TOMB OF THE UNKNOWN SLAVE

What: A monument to honor the memory of the enslaved peoples in Louisiana and the world

Where: Along the right-hand side of Saint Augustine Church, 1210 Governor Nichols St.

Cost: Free

Pro Tip: Please be respectful when taking pictures—the church and community are both very active and protective of their monument.

Chains and manacles hang from this grim monument, but local residents often decorate the ground with candles or flowers, causing a strange juxtaposition. You're most likely to see this phenomenon around "Juneteenth" (June 19), the official commemoration date of the end of slavery in the United States.

the eighteenth and nineteenth centuries) were hung from the larger cross. The ground around the monument was littered with smaller crosses made from chains and wood, indicating the only markers these people might have ever received.

Named the Tomb of the Unknown Slave (patterned after the Tomb of the Unknown Soldier), this grim monument now serves as a powerful memorial for all slaves who were buried without recognition. In the monument's own words: "The Tomb of the Unknown Slave is a constant reminder that we are walking on holy ground. Thus, we cannot consecrate this tomb, because it is already consecrated by many slaves' inglorious deaths bereft of any acknowledgement, dignity or respect, but ultimately glorious by their blood, sweat, tears, faith, prayers, and deep worship of our Creator."

You can pay further respect to the long history of African American heritage in the neighborhood by visiting the Backstreet Cultural Museum, which sits on the same block of Henriette Delille Street as Saint Augustine Church (around the corner from the monument).

THE FIRE UPSTAIRS

What tragic event in the French Quarter galvanized the gay rights movement?

The UpStairs Lounge was well known as a community hub and a welcoming location for both gay men and their allies. The Metropolitan Community Church (the nation's first gay church) even held services there. All that would come to an end on June 24, 1973, when the bar was set ablaze. It was the largest individual attack on an LGBT establishment until the Orlando Pulse shooting in 2016.

The details are still murky even today. It's thought that a male prostitute (upset that he had been ejected from the bar for soliciting) started a fire at the bottom of the stairs to scare the patrons, and then rang the door buzzer to alert the bar. Unfortunately, when the upstairs door was opened, the backdraft sucked the fire up the stairwell and into the lounge, beginning a chain reaction that would eventually claim thirty-two lives.

The reaction by much of the city compounded the tragedy. Neither the mayor nor the archdiocese would ever release a statement. The police refused to investigate, and the crime remains unsolved. Worst of all, some of the victims were never identified by families worrying about

---

The story of the UpStairs Lounge has now been immortalized in two documentaries, *Prejudice and Pride* (2018) and *UpStairs Inferno* (2015); as well as two musicals, *UpStairs* and *The View UpStairs.*

The plaque can be found on Iberville Street, walking away from the Mississippi River toward the back of the Jimani Bar. The words "Unidentified White Male" appear three times, acknowledging the three victims who had still not been identified when the monument was placed (one was finally acknowledged in 2018).

THE UPSTAIRS LOUNGE MEMORIAL

What: A plaque commemorating the site of the most significant tragedy in LGBT New Orleans

Where: 141 Chartres St. (at the corner of Chartres and Iberville)

Cost: Free, though we recommend spending $5 to raise a glass to honor the victims at the Jimani Bar, at the same location on the first floor (as it was in 1973).

Pro Tip: To add your own prayers for the deceased, you can visit Saint Mark's Methodist Church, still in operation. It sits at the top of the French Quarter at 1120 North Rampart St.

the stigma of acknowledging a gay relation.

Nevertheless, the event would serve as a rallying point for the gay rights movement in New Orleans, much in the same way the Stonewall Riots had done for New York City just a few years before. Perhaps the clearest example of this sentiment occurred during the funeral service held for the victims at Saint Mark's Methodist Church. When the press gathered outside the church, mourners were offered the side door as an inconspicuous exit. A woman stood and announced, "I came in through the front, and I'm going to leave through the front."

The congregation—gay and straight alike—followed her.

THE OLD SQUARE COCKTAIL

What is the official cocktail of the French Quarter?

While the official cocktail of New Orleans is the Sazerac, few know about the official cocktail of the French Quarter. Invented in 1938 at the Hotel Monteleone, the Vieux Carré cocktail is a strong and complex cocktail with an interesting name and choice of ingredients.

Vieux Carré in French means old square. It's a term that the Creoles used instead of the term "French Quarter." This cocktail was created by Walter Bergeron at the Hotel Monteleone, and it brings together six ingredients representing the influence of different people of the "Old Square":

Rye whiskey - American
Cognac and Benedictine - French
Angostura and Peychaud's bitters - Caribbean
Vermouth - Italian

Cocktail aficionados will notice that some of the ingredients overlap among the Vieux Carré with the Sazerac and La Louisiane cocktails. While the history of the Sazerac has been studied in depth, it's unclear whether

---

Those seeking both a great Vieux Carré and an education while sipping should visit local cocktail historian Chris McMillian at his bar, Revel, located in the Mid-City neighborhood.

Birthplace of the Vieux Carré Cocktail—the Hotel Monteleone.

The Vieux Carré cocktail

THE OFFICIAL COCKTAIL OF THE FRENCH QUARTER

What: Vieux Carré cocktail

Where: Hotel Monteleone

Cost: $12

Pro Tip: Compare the Vieux Carré with the La Louisiane at the La Louisiane's 21st Amendment Bar just around the corner from the Hotel Monteleone and see which one you prefer!

the Vieux Carré or the La Louisiane came first (and therefore which influenced the other). Regardless, it's a classic that is now served in better cocktail bars around the world.

The Vieux Carré is served over rocks with a cherry. While it is quite potent, it's also quite smooth and therefore a favorite of French Quarter revelers.

COVERING KATRINA

Why can images of the New Orleans water meter be seen on such things as T-shirts and jewelry?

It's easy to spot tourists in New Orleans. They will often be wearing Mardi Gras beads around their necks and the Hand Grenade drink in their hand while walking down Bourbon Street. They also often wear funny T-shirts sold at the countless souvenir shops throughout the French Quarter. But there is one T-shirt design that only locals who have been in New Orleans for quite a while will understand. It's a picture of the New Orleans water meter cover. It can be seen on T-shirts, hats, and even jewelry! Tourists often ask why New Orleanians have such a fascination with the water meters, and there is good reason for it.

The water meter cover shows a crescent moon with stars shooting downward along with the words WATER METER through the center, NEW ORLEANS, LA along the bottom, and SEWERAGE & WATER BOARD CRESCENT BOX across the top. The design of the cover is a favorite among New Orleanians because while it's aesthetically pleasing with the crescent moon symbolizing New Orleans's nickname of "Crescent City," it is also a reminder of Hurricane Katrina.

In 2005, Hurricane Katrina rolled through New Orleans, causing unprecedented flooding—flooding so intense

---

The meter cover and design was created by the Ford Meter Box company out of Wabash, Indiana, in 1921.

Locals adore the water meter iconography. It can be seen everywhere: earrings, coasters, artwork, and even in the tile at the Canal Street entrance to Harrah's Casino.

The New Orleans water meter covers. Notice the crescent moon and stars and the term "Crescent Box."

that the water pushed these metal water meter covers up and often off the hole they covered. The cover became a reminder to locals of the power of Katrina and the water sewerage system which clearly failed.

Sadly, it's hard to find original water meter covers today. Locals have stolen almost all of them and placed them on their walls and picture stands, not to mention EBay. The city has replaced the missing ones with covers that just say "Water" to prevent theft. But that doesn't mean that there are no originals left. Tourists in the know can be found taking pictures of these rare covers and regarding the find as lucky!

NEW ORLEANS WATER METER COVER

What: Reminder of Hurricane Katrina

Where: Various places around New Orleans

Cost: Free

Pro Tip: There ARE some water meter covers that look a lot like the original but aren't. If it doesn't say "New Orleans" and "Crescent Box," then it isn't one of the coveted ones.

WHO DAT

Where can you step through a time machine?

Hint: Ask Brad Pitt!

There are not many places in New Orleans that are dedicated to the city's English ties. In the quaint, village-like atmosphere of Algiers Point, a neighborhood British pub shines like a beacon to Great Britain ex-pats, Anglophiles, and anyone else who just needs a friendly place to grab a pint.

The Crown & Anchor English Pub is a little slice of England in New Orleans. Visitors can easily find it after a quick but picturesque five-minute ferry ride from the French Quarter (which is worth doing in and of itself), followed by a short, two-block stroll.

The blue life-size police box that serves as the bar's entry is instantly recognizable by any sci-fan as a TARDIS time machine from the cult classic TV show *Doctor Who*. Stepping into this TARDIS may not transport people

---

While the TARDIS and interior artifacts are draw enough, it's the people who really make the visit special. This neighborhood watering hole is as welcoming to tourists as it is to their regulars. But be warned—while many intend to pop in for one, they often find themselves not emerging until hours later, having had remarkable conversations and story swapping with a dozen new "old friends" they just met.

The life-size Doctor Who *TARDIS serves as the Crown & Anchor English Pub's entrance.*

CROWN & ANCHOR ENGLISH PUB

What: A *Doctor Who* TARDIS

Where: 200 Pelican Ave.

Cost: Free

Pro Tip: The bar itself is for those 21 and older, but all ages are welcome to sit at the picnic tables outside.

through time, but they will apparently travel through space—entering from New Orleans and emerging in London.

The pub interior is a collection of British-related memorabilia, complete with imported English beers and cider on draft, a dartboard, and England-made snacking "crisps." The atmosphere is so authentic that it has been host to many movie scenes that are supposed to take place in Great Britain. For 2015's *The Big Short*, the crew did not change a thing in order to film Brad Pitt's London pub scene. You can even sit at the same two-seater round table he used, which is just through the entrance on the left, closest to the staircase.

TRAVELING THE WORLD ONE GLASS AT A TIME

Where can one taste wines from various countries in one visit?

New Orleans is known for cocktails but not so much for wine. Even so, there is one special place for wine lovers. Tucked away in the Warehouse District with an unassuming storefront is a wine bar unlike anything else in New Orleans. For those wishing to taste wine from around the world, one need only seek out W.I.N.O. The acronym stands for Wine Institute of New Orleans, and this wine heaven doesn't disappoint. Upon entering, the cashier takes the guest's credit card and hands them a wine glass and a data card. Guests now have the freedom to receive tastes or full glasses of wine from around the world. The walls of W.I.N.O. are lined with taps lit with three buttons at each bottle. Each tap is connected to a different bottle, and the bottles are arranged by country. One can choose to push the small-, medium-, or full-pour button from any (and as many!) bottles as they like and will be charged accordingly at the end of their visit. Patrons range from serious wine connoisseurs to those just looking for a fun night out with friends.

THE WINE INSTITUTE OF NEW ORLEANS

What: A wine lover's paradise with 120 wines on tap!

Where: 610 Tchoupitoulas St.

Cost: \$-\$\$ Dependent on how much one drinks.

Pro Tip: Those wishing to eat a little something while they imbibe should check out their cheese plates.

Top: W.I.N.O. on Tchoupitoulas Street.
Right: The wine taps are organized by country and then by style. Follow the line of taps into the back room where there are tables and more obscure styles.

Visitors entering for the first time think that what they initially see is the entire venue. What they later learn is that it's only the front room. The line of taps stretches down a hall and into a back area with even more taps and more room for seating.

GUMBO ISN'T THE ONLY FAMOUS SOUP IN NOLA

What comfort food is finding fame in NOLA?

What served as sustenance for the poor in the past is often considered a delicacy today. Take red beans and rice or grits, for example. Once made to feed poor enslaved people, these dishes bring in a pretty penny in finer establishments today. Another such dish is a lesser-known soup that for many years could only be found in a neighbor's kitchen, corner groceries, or small restaurants—*Ya-Ka-Mein*. *Ya-Ka-Mein* is a spicy, beef-brothy soup made with spaghetti noodles, green onions, boiled egg, beef, lots of black pepper, and sometimes shrimp. Locals add hot sauce and/or soy sauce to the already salty broth for a real kick.

While there are differing opinions on the origin of the soup, one theory is the most prevalent. New Orleans had two different Chinatowns at different times in history. One sprang up after the Civil War near Tulane Avenue and Elk Place. The second emerged just before World War II on Bourbon Street. In the latter Chinatown, Chinese food began fusing with Creole cuisine and into the psyche of Creole cooks. *Ya-Ka-Mein* was a delicious soup that was cheap to make and easy to take home.

If you can't find Mrs. Linda's *Ya-Ka-Mein*, visit Bywater Bakery, which often has the soup daily until 2 p.m.

Ya-Ka-Mein *with shrimp at Jazz Fest.*

YA-KA-MEIN

What: A salty, peppery soup with meat, egg, green onions, and spaghetti noodles

Where: Various festivals

Cost: $3–$6 for a cup depending on where it is found

Pro Tip: *Ya-Ka-Mein* has been a favorite hangover remedy in New Orleans. There always seems to be a festival somewhere where one can find some.

Although one can find *Ya-Ka-Mein* in restaurants today, it is rare. A better chance of finding it is at one of the many festivals held annually in New Orleans. One such festival is Jazz Fest, where Ms. Linda Green ladles out her *Ya-Ka-Mein* to the masses who can't seem to get enough. Ms. Linda (a.k.a. the *Ya-Ka-Mein* Lady) won recognition on the Food Network's *Chopped* TV show has been featured on numerous other foodie shows.

YES, YOU MAY

Where can you see a legal license for prostitution?

The Creole cottage and French Quarter bar that now carries the name "May Baily's Place" dates back to 1821. Records show that famed naturalist John James Audubon created his *Birds of America* series while sitting in that very cottage the same year it was built. A manor was added in 1834, which later became a convent that was used as a hospital for Union soldiers during the Civil War. But the time period leading up to the war is perhaps the most fascinating.

All port cities were known for a certain amount of debauchery. Young male dockhands and sailors were paid upon arrival and promptly spent that money on young men's pursuits. New Orleans was no different. May Baily and her sister, Millie, were orphaned shortly after arriving from Ireland and settled in the little cottage that now carries May's name. With little money and no skills, the sisters took advantage of the seemingly unrelenting

---

Prostitution was legal for twenty years until Storyville was officially shut down on November 12, 1917. Its demise began two years earlier, at the beginning of WWI, when the US Navy ordered all vice districts within a five-mile radius of a naval base to be closed. Apparently, too many sailors were contracting "companionship" diseases during their visits to Storyville.

No. 19. LICENSE

Mayoralty of New-Orleans

City Hall 30th day of May 1857

Miss May Baily

Having paid the Tax imposed by Ordinance No. 3267 concerning Lewd and Abandoned Women she is hereby authorized to occupy until 31st January 1858 the second or other than the first floor of the building of dwelling situated on Dauphine street No. 423 between St. Louis street and Conti street

Provided the provisions of the aforesaid Ordinance in all its particulars be complied with

Chas. M. Waterman Mayor

Left: The back room of May Baily's.
Right: The license, showing that the tax was paid for "Lewd and Abandoned Women," as prostitutes were then considered.

PROSTITUTION LICENSE

What: The actual document issued to May Baily making prostitution legal at her bordello

Where: May Baily's Place, 415 Dauphine St.

Cost: Free

Pro Tip: Excellent cocktails are available at the bar.

demand for prostitution and turned their cottage and the adjacent building into a successful bordello.

The city officials began fining these houses of ill repute daily as a means to squelch their scandalous activities. Undeterred, May Baily offered to pay this fine in advance, knowing the city's attempt was sure to fail. And fail it did. The city became resigned to a truce of sorts and began issuing licenses instead of fines. Plucky May Baily became the proud owner of the first licensed brothel in the city on May 30, 1857. Today, the license remains hanging on the wall in an unassuming frame. Its crumpled appearance bears witness to the hotly disputed industry.

Eventually, a larger attempt was made to restrict these activities into a designated red-light district. It was nicknamed "Storyville" after the city council president, Sidney Story, who championed it in order to keep closer tabs on the sordid activities of the gambling dens, honky-tonks, and brothels.

SOURCES

Allan, M. Carrie. "This Classic Cocktail is also an Arm Workout—If You Want One." *The Washington Post*. April 9, 2019.

Andrews, Evan. "Why is the South known as 'Dixie?'" History.com. June 8, 2017.

AngelOfTheDelta.org. "Margaret's Bakery Photos," n.d.

Anson, Tylyn. Personal Interview. May 13, 2019.

Arnaud's Restaurant. "Lagniappe." www.arnaudsrestaurant.com/about/lagniappe.

Arnaud's Restaurant. "Mardi Gras Museum." www.arnaudsrestaurant.com/about/mardi-gras-museum.

Asher, Sally. "Last Days of Storyville." MyNewOrleans.com. www.myneworleans.com/last-days-of-storyville. September 9, 2017.

Bar Tonique. "Menu." www.bartonique.com.

Beauvais, Constance. "The First and Last Days of Paul Morphy." Unpublished, n.d.

Biography.com Editors. "Jimmy Buffett Biography." www.biography.com/musician/jimmy-buffett. August 12, 2019.

Branley, Edward. "History of the Casket Girls of New Orleans." GoNola.com. October 16, 2018.

Branley, Edward. "NOLA History: The Old Ursuline Convent in the French Quarter." *GoNola.com*. March 30, 2011.

Brister, Nancy. "The Old Lighthouse for the Blind Building." www.old-new-orleans.com/NO_Lighthouse.html, n.d.

Bruno, R. Stephanie. "Falstaff brewery sign will shine again." *Nola.com* (January, 10 2011), www.nola.com/news/business/article_cacc19fe-2a30-5f8d-9ace-2ed8dea36279.html.

Bruno, R. Stephanie. "Former French Quarter brothel becomes home sweet home." *Nola.com* (November 13, 2011), www.nola.com/homegarden/2011/11/former_french_quarter_brothel.html.

Campanella, Richard. "Tunnel vision: In 1966, New Orleans Built a Tunnel Downtown Hoping the Traffic Would Come." Nola.com, October 8, 2014.

Catahoula Hotel. "Piscobar at Catahoula." www.catahoulahotel.com/pisco-bar.

Catholic Online. "St. Expeditus." www.catholic.org/saints/saint.php?saint_id=347. Accessed February 2, 2019.

Chalmers, J.P. "Rock, Smith and Blackton Were Pioneers." *The Moving Picture World*. New York: Chalmers Publishing Company, July 15, 1916.

Charming, Cheryl. The Cocktail Companion. Coral Gables: Mango Publishing. November 30, 2018.

Clifford, Catherine. "134-year-old Oyster Company Stops Shucking." *CNN Money*, June 12, 2010.

Congdon, Kristin G. & Hallmark, Kelley Kara. "Southeastern Regional Artists: Charles Gillam Sr." *American Folk Art: A Regional Reference, Volume 1*. Kristin G. Congdon and Kara Kelley Hallmark, 2012.

Contributing writer. "It Wasn't McIlhenny's Fault, and Other Things to Know About Nutria in Louisiana." *The Times-Picayune*. April 26, 2017.

Cooper, Christopher. "Louisiana Is Trying To Turn a Pest Into a Meal." *The New York Times*, December 14, 1997.

Coyle, Cathal. "Oliver Pollock – the Irishman who created the US $ sign." *Ireland's Own*, June 21, 2016.

Cush, Andy. "The Wildest Venue in New Orleans Is a Musical Village, Where Every House Is an Instrument." *Spin Magazine*, November 18, 2016.

Cutler, Charles L. "Paul Morphy, Chess Prodigy." *American Heritage*. August 1972. Vol. 23, Issue 5.

Cvitanovich, Tommy. Interview. Drago's Seafood Restaurant. October 5, 2016.

Danger, Tatiana. "Witchcraft, cotton and ghosts: The real story of New Orleans' Buckner Mansion." *Roadtrippers*, February 1, 2016, www.roadtrippers.com/stories/buckner-mansion.

Dauphine Orleans. "May Baily's Place." www.dauphineorleans.com/nightlife, n.d.

Difford, Simon. "Ramos Gin Fizz Cocktail." *Difford's Guide*, n.d.

Dowling, Dija. "Video: Meet the Artist Behind City Park's 'Singing Oak' Tree." *Very Local New Orleans*, October 23, 2019.

Drago's Seafood Restaurant. www.dragosrestaurant.com/about/our-oysters. Accessed January 5, 2019.

Eiffel Society. www.eiffelsociety.com/our-history, n.d.

Espina, Marina E. *Filipinos in Louisiana*. New Orleans: A.F. Laborde & Sons. 1998.

Ever, Owen. Interview. New Orleans Pharmacy Museum. 2018.

Farris, Teresa Parker with Ornelas, Rachel. "'One Option Out of Many': Strategies for Preserving Louisiana Folk Culture in the Twenty-first Century." *Folklife in Louisiana*. Louisiana Division of the Arts, 2013.

Ferrand, Casey. "Woman steals iconic water meter covers uptown." WDSU news, April 17, 2017.

Fleming, Colin. "Fifty years after John Kennedy Toole died, 'A Confederacy of Dunces' lives on." *The Washington Post*, March 26, 2019.

Florence, Robert. "Barbarin musical dynasty invites musicians to share family tomb." *Preservation in Print* [New Orleans, LA], May 26, 2005.

Fradin, Dennis Brindell. *The Louisiana Purchase*. Benchmark Books, 2009.

Francis, Sylvester. Interview. Backstreet Cultural Museum. November 2017.

Frasier, Jim. *The Garden District of New Orleans*. Jackson, MS: University Press of Mississippi, 2012.

French, Gerald. Interview. The Original Tuxedo Dixieland Jazz Band. June 14, 2019.

Gajus, Gregory. Interview. Mr. Gregory's Shrimp Boil. January 14, 2019.

Gastelum, Pandora. Personal Interview. May 14, 2019.

Gerdes, Caroline. "Understanding The Katrina 'X'." *National Geographic*, 17 August 2012, blog.nationalgeographic.org/2012/08/17/understanding-the-katrina-x. Accessed April 22, 2019.

Gilbert, Jim & Gilbert, Lisa. "Perley A. Thomas Then lent His Expertise to Thomas Built Buses Inc." *The Chatham Daily News*, December 1, 2017.

Gillis, James. Interview. MS Rau Antiques. April 2019.

Gisclair, S. Derby. "Lords of the Ring." *MyNewOrleans.com*, November 27, 2013.

Glassman, Sallie Ann. "International Shrine of Marie Laveau at the New Orleans Healing Center." *NewOrleans.com*, October 31, 2017, www.neworleans.com/articles/post/international-shrine-of-marie-laveau-at-the-new-orleans-healing-center. Accessed February 13, 2019.

Godoy, Maria. "Meet The Calas, A New Orleans Tradition That Helped Free Slaves." *National Public Radio*, February 12, 2013.

Gonzales, Ph.D., Randy. Interview. Filipinos in New Orleans. June 9, 2019.

Guion, William. *Quercus Louisiana: The Splendid Live Oaks of Louisiana*. New Orleans, LA: William Guion Photographs, 2019.

Gumbo Shop. "About us." www.gumboshop.com/history.php.

Guste, Roy. *Antoine's Restaurant Since 1840: 175th Anniversary Celebration*. Roy Guste: 2014.

Halm, Joseph. "'Storyteller,' 'magician' Andrew Higgins remembered at WWII museum by family." *nola.com*, November 10, 2017. www.nola.com/archive/article_ed794ec5-70fe-5667-960d-9d907286aab9.html.

Hambrick, Keith S. "The Swedish Nightingale in New Orleans: Jenny Lind's Visit of 1851." *Louisiana History: The Journal of the Louisiana Historical Association* (Autumn 1981), Vol. 22, No. 4.

Haydel's Bakery. "Russian Cake." www.haydelsbakery.com/russian-cake. Accessed June 25, 2019.

Heard, Malcolm. *French Quarter Manual: An Architectural Guide to New Orleans Vieux Carré*. Jackson: University Press of Mississippi. 1997.

Hémard, Ned. "Championship of Kenner." *New Orleans Nostalgia*, 2018, www.neworleansbar.org/uploads/files/Championship%20in%20Kenner%201_3_18.pdf.

Hémard, Ned. "Minit Made." *New Orleans Nostalgia*, 2013, www.neworleansbar.org/uploads/files/Minit%20Made%202-27.pdf.

Hémard, Ned. "New Orleans Nostalgia: Skating Through History." *New Orleans Nostalgia*, 2014, www.neworleansbar.org/uploads/files/Skating%20Through%20History_3-26.pdf.

Hicks, Peter. "Louisiana: To Have and Have Not…" *Fondation Napoléon*, www.napoleon.org/en/history-of-the-two-empires/articles/louisiana-to-have-and-to-have-not. Accessed May 1, 2019.

Horning, Katrina. “The Rink Myth Debunked!” *New Orleans Architectural Tours*, August 13, 2018.

Hotel Monteleone. “The Historic Carousel Bar,” www.hotelmonteleone.com/entertainment/carousel-bar. Accessed May 18, 2019.

H. Rault Locksmith. “The second oldest locksmith in the United States.” www.hrault.com. Accessed April 10, 2019.

International Boxing Hall of Fame. “Corbett Was King of New Era,” www.ibhof.com/pages/archives/corbettsullivan.html, n.d.

Jochum, Kimberly. “Dueling Oak.” New Orleans Historical, www.neworleanshistorical.org/items/show/109. Accessed July 23, 2019.

Karst, James. “Houdini escaped from a straitjacket high above Canal street.” *Nola.com*, February 28, 2016.

Kemp, Charlotte. “Miss Josie Arlington and Her Haunted Tomb.” *Paranormal Hauntings*, 1 October 2018, www.paranormalhauntings.blog/2018/10/01/miss-josie-arlington-and-her-haunted-tomb. Accessed March 28, 2019.

Kennedy, J. Michael. “He Doesn’t Want Name Blackened: Cajun Food Frenzy Snares Little Fish and a Big Chef.” *Los Angeles Times*, August 11, 1986.

Kennon, Alexandra. *Classic Restaurants of New Orleans*. Charleston: The History Press, 2019.

Kesler, Kevin. “The Many Types of BBQ Sauces in the United States.” *The Cookful*, n.d.

Kluth, Megan. “Napoleon Bonaparte’s death mask was almost thrown out with the trash.” www.WGNO.com. January 18, 2017.

Lanier, Clint and Derek Hembree. “Tracking Down the Best Dive Bar in New Orleans.” *The Huffington Post*, September 9, 2013.

Larson, Susan. “William Faulkner house in New Orleans has a story in every room.” *Nola.com*, November 7, 2009.

Lawrence, Christina. “St. Augustine Catholic Church.” New Orleans Historical, www.neworleanshistorical.org/items/show/551. Accessed March 23, 2019.

Leach, Christopher. “The not so secret, secret room of M.S. Rau antiques.” www.WGNO.com, December 31, 2018.

LeGardeur, Lili. “Grand Finale.” *Gambit* [New Orleans, LA], August 2, 2004.

Lehrman Institute. “The Louisiana Purchase,” www.lehrmaninstitute.org/history/louisiana-purchase.html. Accessed April 29, 2019.

Le Musée de f.p.c. “Our Story,” www.lemuseedefpc.com/ourstory. Accessed June 8, 2019.

Levees.org, “London Avenue Canal Levee Breach in 2005.” New Orleans Historical, www.neworleanshistorical.org/items/show/276. Accessed April 13, 2019.

LighthouseFriends. “Port Pontchartrain Lighthouse, Louisiana,” www.lighthousefriends.com/light.asp?ID=807, n.d. Accessed June 17, 2019.

Lighthouse Louisiana. “About,” www.lighthouselouisiana.org. Accessed July 2, 2019.

Looby, Caitlin. "Nutria Bounty (Yes, the Nutria Bounty) in Louisiana Rises after 'Uptake in Damage'" *New Orleans Advocate*, June 30, 2019.

Lopez, Kenny. "The story of the 'American Horror Story' mansion in New Orleans." *News With a Twist*, WGNO New Orleans, November 7, 2018. www.wgno.com/2018/11/07/the-story-of-the-american-horror-story-mansion-in-new-orleans.

Louisiana Writers' Project. *New Orleans City Park: its first fifty years*. New Orleans, LA: Gulf Print Co., 1941.

Love, Bret. "These are the Mardi Gras Indians of New Orleans." *National Geographic*, March 9, 2016.

MacCash, Doug. "Banksy's 'Umbrella Girl' covered with plywood and under guard." *Nola.com*, February 22, 2014, www.nola.com/arts/2014/02/banksys_umbrella_girl_seems_to.html.

MacCash, Doug. "Chewbacchus and Dat Dog Team Up for Silly Mardi Gras Shrine Room." *The Times-Picayune*, February 3, 2017.

Marcus, Frances Frank. "New Orleans's 'Eiffel Tower'," *New York Times*, December 10, 1986, p. C18.

Market Street Railway. "No. 952 New Orleans, Louisiana," www.streetcar.org/streetcars/952-952-new-orleans-desire. Accessed June 28, 2019.

Marshmallowmagpie. "The New Orleans Crescent Meter Box," www.marshmallowmagpie.wordpress.com/2016/05/26/the-new-orleans-crescent-meter-box/comment-page-1. Accessed May 26, 2016.

Martin, Addie K. & Martin, Jeremy. *Southeast Louisiana Food*. Charleston: American Palate, 2014.

Mardi Gras World, "Our History," www.mardigrasworld.com/about-us/our-history. Accessed March 1, 2019.

Mariano, Allie. "A 'Eureka' moment: How Andrew Higgins landed himself on the U.S. Navy's radar." *The Times-Picayune*, June 4, 2017.

Massa, Dominic. "50 Years Ago Today: Victory in the Fight Against a Vieux Carre Riverfront Expressway." www.WWLTV.com, July 1, 2019.

McCollam, Julie. "Bywater: Still Mecca For The Unconventional." *Preservation In Print* (May 2005), Vol. 32, No. 4.

McKnight, Laura. "City Diner's a la carte pancake is a pizza-size crowd-pleaser." *The Times Picayune*, September 28, 2012.

McMillian, Chris. Interview. "Vieux Carré Cocktail." March 27, 2019.

Mizell-Nelson, Michael. "The Elusive History of the New Orleans Russian Cake." *Louisiana Cultural Vistas*. Louisiana Endowment for the Humanities: Winter 2012.

M.S. Rau Antiques. "GONOLA.com See & Do video: Explore the secret room at M.S. Rau Antiques," www.rauantiques.com/blog/gonola-com-video-explore-secret-room-m-s-rau-antiques. Accessed June 3, 2019.

Muriels.com. "Our Ghost." www.muriels.com/about/ghost. Accessed June 14, 2019.

Music Box Village. www.musicboxvillage.com. Accessed April 21, 2019.

My Airport Trip. "Why MSY for Louis Armstrong New Orleans Airport," www.myairporttrip.com/blog/new-orleans/why-msy-for-luis-armstrong-new-orleans-international-airport, n.d. Accessed July 3, 2019.

New Orleans & Co. "New Orleans Snowballs," www.neworleansonline.com/neworleans/cuisine/cuisines/snowballs.html. Accessed May 31, 2019.

New Orleans City Park. "Big Lake," www.neworleanscitypark.com/in-the-park/big-lake. Accessed May 5, 2019.

New Orleans Ghosts. "Dining with the darkness: The curious table at Muriel's Jackson Square." www.nolaghosts.com/muriels-jackson-square. Accessed May 3, 2019.

Nola Gondola. "About," www.nolagondola.com. Accessed June 1, 2019.

Old New Orleans."Mr. Moisant's fateful visit." OldNewOrleans.com. www.old-new-orleans.com/NO_Moisant.html, n.d.

Osborne, Terrance. Interview. 2018.

Ousset, Matthew. Interview. Antoine's Restaurant. 2016.

P. & J. Oyster Company, Inc. "History of P&J Oyster Company," www.oysterlover.com/about. Accessed April 29, 2019.

Padgett, Charles Stephen. "Jimmy Buffett." *The Encyclopedia of Alabama*, July 13, 2007.

Pascal's Manale. "Our History," www.pascalsmanale.com/history. Accessed May 2, 2019.

Pontchartrain, Blake. "Blakeview: the Falstaff weather ball" *Gambit* [New Orleans, LA], August 3, 2015.

Ponchartrain, Blake. "Blakeview: The Simon Bolivar Statue." *Gambit* [New Orleans, LA], November 21, 2017.

Ponchartrain, Blake. "What happened to the remains of Josie Arlington, the Storyville madam?" *Gambit* [New Orleans, LA], November 23, 2015.

Ponchartrain, Blake. "Where exactly in City Park are the Dueling Oaks and the Suicide Oak?" *Gambit* [New Orleans, LA], February 8, 2016.

Ponchartrain, Blake. "Who Started Painting Those Colorful Plank Signs With Sayings First, Dr. Bob Or Simon?" *The Gambit*, July 21, 2014.

Ponchartrain, Blake. "Why Do They Call It the Rink?" *The Gambit*, October 29, 2018.

Pope, John. "Nearly 200 Years Later, St. Charles Avenue Streetcar Line Still Rings New Orleans' Bell," *The Times-Picayune*, January 11, 2017.

Primeaux, Sam. "The Original Tuxedo Jazz Band: What's in a Name?" *Offbeat Magazine*, January 1, 2012.

Ramsey, Jan. "Jimmy Buffett on Bourbon Street," *Offbeat Magazine*, May 11, 2011.

Reckdahl, Katy. "Descendants Tell Stories of Free People of Color," *The New York Times*, March 12, 2019.

Reed, Dale Volberg, John Shelton Reed, and Brett Anderson. "The Natural." *Cornbread Nation 4: The Best of Southern Food Writing*. Athens: University of Georgia Press, May 15, 2008.

Regua, Michael. Interview. Antoine's Restaurant. 2018.

Ringle, Ken. "The Boat That Sank Hitler," *The Washington Post*, May 29, 2000.

Rivera, Jenidza. "Faulkner's House." *New Orleans Historical*. www.neworleanshistorical.org/items/show/1396. Accessed April 23, 2019.

RoadsideAmerica.com. "Statue of Ignatius J. Reilly." www.roadsideamerica.com/story/18313, n.d.

Roe, Ken. "Vitascope Hall." Cinema Treasures. www.cinematreasures.org/theaters/42202. Accessed June 10, 2019.

Roesgen, Susan. "Peer inside the Katrina 'Flooded House Museum'," *WGNO.com*, April 7, 2019, www.wgno.com/2019/04/07/peer-inside-the-katrina-flooded-house-museum.

Rothman, Joshua D. "The curious origins of the dollar sign." www.werehistory.org. April 1, 2018.

Ross, Janell. "The art — and controversy — of Hurricane Katrina 'X-codes'," *The Washington Post*, August 29, 2015.

Sarah. "American Horror Story's Buckner Mansion In New Orleans." *HouseCrazy*, 2013. www.house-crazy.com/american-horror-storys-buckner-mansion-in-new-orleans.

Scott, Mike. "The (almost) true legend of St. Expedite in New Orleans." *The Times-Picayune* [New Orleans, LA], August 19, 2017.

Scott, Mike. "1952: Falstaff gets into the forecasting business with its 'weather ball'." *The Times-Picayune* [New Orleans, LA], October 22, 2017.

Scott, Mike. "The Story of Canal Street's Vitascope Hall, the World's First Movie Theater." *The Times-Picayune*. June 18, 2017.

Senfy, Paul. "Rum stories: The history of the Hurricane." *Distiller*. March 4, 2018.

Silverman, Emily. "The St. Louis Exchange Hotel and the New Orleans." *Via Nola Vie*. December 13, 2017.

Spera, Keith. "At age 90, master float builder Blaine Kern is a more mellow Mr. Mardi Gras." *The Advocate* [New Orleans, LA], February 3, 2018.

Staff. "Entrepreneur Spotlight: Robert Dula of NOLA Gondola." *InTheNola.com*, April 21, 2014. http://www.inthenola.com/local-spotlights/entrepreneurs/item/2081-entrepreneur-spotlight-robert-dula-of-nola-gondola.

Staff. "July 4th: Soul of America—Interview with Charles Gillam." *American Routes*. WWNO.org, July 2, 2003.

Staff. "Ms. Linda's Original Ya-Ka-Mein." *Louisiana Kitchen*. January 1, 2017.

Staff. "Edward Douglass White, 1910–1921." *The Supreme Court Historical Society*, n.d.

Sunseri, Alfred. Interview. P&J's Oyster Company. June 17, 2019.

Taylor, Michael. "Free People of Color in Louisiana: Revealing an Unknown Past." LSU Libraries, Collaborative Digital Collection. www.lib.lsu.edu/sites/all/files/sc/fpoc/history.html, n.d.

Terrance Osborne. "About." www.terranceosborne.com/about.

"The man who won World War II." *Retropod* from *The Washington Post*, June 6, 2017, www.soundcloud.com/washington-post/the-man-who-won-world-war-ii.

"The Tree of Life." *Atlas Obscura*, www.atlasobscura.com/places/the-tree-of-life-2-new-orleans-louisiana. Accessed March 22, 2019.

Thomas, Jabari. "Napoleon signed the Louisiana Purchase in a tub. Now you can bathe in it!" *News With a Twist,* uploaded by WGNO New Orleans, November 16, 2015. www.wgno.com/2015/11/16/napoleon-signed-the-louisiana-purchase-in-a-tub-now-you-can-bathe-in-it.

"Tomb of the Unknown Slave." *Atlas Obscura*, www.atlasobscura.com/places/tomb-of-the-unknown-slave. Accessed April 4, 2019.

Timms, Neil. Interview. Crown & Anchor English Pub. June 8, 2019.

Tujague's Restaurant. "History." www.tujaguesrestaurant.com/history.

Tujague's Restaurant. "Tujague's history: the Birthplace of Brunch." www.tujaguesrestaurant.com/news-and-events/tujagues-history-birthplace-of-brunch.

Turkel, CMHS, ISHC, Stanley. *Built to Last: 100+ Year-Old Hotels East of the Mississippi*. Bloomington: AuthorHouse. September 18, 2013.

Urban Dictionary. "Huck-a-buck," www.urbandictionary.com/define.php?term=huck-a-buck, n.d.

Vargas, Ramon Antonio. "Drago Cvitanovich, Co-Founder of Legendary Metairie Seafood Restaurant Drago's, Dies at 94." *The New Orleans Advocate*. February 4, 2017.

Vella, Christina. *Intimate Enemies*. Baton Rouge: Louisiana State University Press, 1997.

Wann, Tyler. "Step inside Snake and Jake's Christmas Lounge, the New Orleans dive bar where it's Christmas year-round." *Nola.com*, December 24, 2014. www.nola.com/entertainment_life/article_77c591bf-dbd7-575d-a65b-421495101431.html.

Welch, Michael Patrick. "NOLA Filipino History Stretches for Centuries." *New Orleans. Me Journal*. October 27, 2014.

Westbrook, Laura. "Mabuhay Pilipino! (Long Life!): Filipino Culture in Southeast Louisiana." *Folklife in Louisiana*. Baton Rouge: Louisiana Folklife Program. 2008.

What's Cooking America. "Oysters Rockefeller Recipe and History." www.whatscookingamerica.net/Seafood/OystersRockefeller.htm, n.d.

Widmer, Mary Lou. Margaret, *Friend Of Orphans*. Charleston: Arcadia Publishing. October 31, 1996.

Williams, Karen. "St. Expedito's Role in South Louisiana Catholicism. *In Louisiana Folklore Miscellany*, Volume 21, 100–110, Louisiana Folklore Society, 2011.

Wiltz, Chris. *The Last Madam*. Boston, Da Capo Press, 1999.

Wine Institute New Orleans (WINO), www.winoschool.com. Accessed July 1, 2019.

Yip, Randall. "Filipino American History: First Asian American Settlement to Receive New Recognition." *AsAmNews*. October 3, 2019.

INDEX